THE NEW CENTRAL ASIA: IN SEARCH OF STABILITY

A Report to
The Trilateral Commission

Authors: SHERMAN W. GARNETT
Dean, James Madison College, Michigan State
University; former Senior Associate, Carnegie
Endowment for International Peace; former U.S.
Deputy Assistant Secretary of Defense for Russia,
Ukraine, and Eurasia

ALEXANDER RAHR
Program Director for Eastern Europe and Head of the
Körber Foundation Unit for Russian and CIS Studies,
German Council on Foreign Relations (DGAP)

KOJI WATANABE
Executive Advisor, Japan Federation of Economic
Organizations; Senior Fellow, Japan Center for
International Exchange; former Japanese Ambassador
to Russia, Kyrgyzstan, Tajikistan, Turkmenistan,
Azerbaijan, Armenia, and Georgia

published by
The Trilateral Commission
New York, Paris, and Tokyo
October 2000

The Trilateral Commission was formed in 1973 by private citizens of Europe, Japan, and North America to foster closer cooperation among these three democratic industrialized regions on common problems. It seeks to improve public understanding of such problems, to support proposals for handling them jointly, and to nurture habits and practices of working together.

© Copyright, 2000. The Trilateral Commission
All Rights Reserved.

Garnett, Sherman W., 1955–
    The new Central Asia: in search of stability: a report to the
    Trilateral Commission/
authors, Sherman W. Garnett, Alexander Rahr, Koji Watanabe
        p. c.m. – (Triangle papers; 54)
    ISBN 0-930503-79-1 (pbk.)
        1. Asia, Central–Foreign Relations–1991– 2. Caucasus–Foreign
    Relations–20th Century. 3. Asia, Central–Economic conditions–
    1991– 4. Caucasus–Economic conditions–20th century. I. Rahr,
    Alexander, 1959– II. Watanabe, Koji, 1934– III. Title. IV. Series.

DK859.57 .G37 2000
327.58–dc21

                                                              00-044306

Manufactured in the United States of America

THE TRILATERAL COMMISSION

345 East 46th Street   c/o Japan Center for   5, rue de Téhéran
New York, NY 10017   International Exchange   75008 Paris, France
                          4-9-17 Minami-Azabu
                                Minato-ku
                            Tokyo 106, Japan

The Authors

SHERMAN W. GARNETT is the Dean of James Madison College, a residential college devoted to the study of public affairs, at Michigan State University. From 1994 to 1999, he was a Senior Associate at the Carnegie Endowment for International Peace, specializing in the foreign and security policies of Russia, Ukraine, and other states created out of the former USSR. From 1983 to 1994, Dr. Garnett served in the U.S. government, ultimately as the Deputy Assistant Secretary of Defense for Russia, Ukraine, and Eurasia (1992–94). Earlier posts in the Defense Department included Director of the Offices for Russia, Ukraine, and Eurasia (1992–93) and for European Security Negotiations (1989–92). Dr. Garnett received his Ph.D. in Russian Literature from the University of Michigan in 1982. He has an M.A. in Russian and East European Studies from Yale University and a B.A. in Political Philosophy from James Madison College at Michigan State University. He has published widely in U.S. and international journals and written or edited several books, including most recently *Getting it Wrong: Regional Cooperation and the Commonwealth of Independent States* (1999, with Martha Brill Olcott and Anders Åslund).

ALEXANDER RAHR, based in Berlin, is both Program Director for Eastern Europe and Head of the Körber Foundation Unit for Russian and CIS Affairs at the German Council on Foreign Relations (DGAP). Educated in history and political science at the Munich State University, he began his career as co-author of a project on the Soviet elite at the Federal Institute for East European and International Studies in Cologne (1977–82). From 1982 to 1994 he was a Research Analyst at the Research Institute of Radio Free Europe/Radio Liberty in Munich. During these years he was also a Political Consultant of the Rand Corporation in Santa Monica, California, and the Council of Europe, Strasbourg. In 1990–91 he was a Fellow at the Soviet Parliament in Moscow and the Institute for East–West Security Studies in New York. From 1994 to 1995 he headed a project on Russian–Ukrainian relations at the German Council on Foreign Relations. He works as commentator for German TV and radio stations, is author of many monographs and articles on Soviet, Russian, and CIS affairs, and is author of biographies of Vladimir Putin (2000) and Mikhail Gorbachev (1986).

KOJI WATANABE is Executive Advisor to the Japan Federation of Economic Organizations (Keidanren) and Senior Fellow at the Japan Center for International Exchange. Ambassador Watanabe has had a very distinguished career in the Japanese Foreign Ministry. He was Ambassador to Russia in 1993–96—also accredited to Kyrgyzstan, Tajikistan, Turkmenistan, Azerbaijan, Armenia, and Georgia—and Ambassador to Italy in 1992–93. Before serving in Rome and Moscow, he was Deputy Minister for Foreign Affairs and while Deputy Minister served as Sherpa for the G-7 Houston and London summits of 1991 and 1990, and Japanese co-chairman of the U.S.–Japan Structural Impediments Initiative Talks. Ambassador Watanabe joined the Foreign Ministry upon graduating from the University of Tokyo in 1956. He was a Visiting Fellow at the Woodrow Wilson School of Princeton University (1957–58) and at the Center for International Affairs of Harvard University (1973–74). His other overseas posts included Counsellor at the Japanese Embassy in Saigon (1974–76), Minister at the Japanese Embassy in Beijing (1981–84), and Ambassador to Saudi Arabia (1988–89). Ambassador Watanabe is a member of the Board of Governors of the Asia-Europe Foundation (ASEF), President of The Japan Forum, and a member of the National Public Safety Commission. His recent publications incude *Engaging Russia in Asia Pacific* (1999).

The Trilateral Process

Among the five chapters of the following report, the opening and closing chapters are the joint responsibility of the three authors. Each author is individually responsible for the particular chapter relating to his country or region.

The initial meetings of the authors, to discuss the overall framework of their report, were on March 15 and 16, 1999, in Washington, D.C., alongside the 1999 annual meeting of the Trilateral Commission. Rahr and Watanabe met in Copenhagen on October 27, 1999. Rahr and Garnett met in Washington, D.C., on January 6–8, 2000. Draft materials for all of the chapters were on the table for detailed discussion when the three authors met in London on March 5–6, 2000. A full draft of the report was completed in late March for discussion at the 2000 annual meeting of the Trilateral Commission, on April 8–10 in Tokyo. Final revisions for publication were completed in August and September.

Consultations have been carried on in each Trilateral area. Consultations in Europe were particularly extensive. In September 1999, Rahr traveled to London, Brussels (EU and NATO), and Paris. In October, he (and Watanabe) consulted with Danish experts. In February 2000, he traveled to Rome. Rahr consulted with a number of relevant persons in Germany. He traveled again to NATO headquarters in Belgium. In July 1999, Watanabe gathered together in Tokyo a number of Japanese experts and others related to the region. He spoke later with various individuals in and out of the Japanese government. In addition to individual discussions with relevant Americans and Canadians, Garnett (and Rahr) consulted with American experts and others related to the region in the Washington, D.C., area in January 2000. Rahr talked with a number of persons during regular trips to Moscow. In late May 2000 he traveled to Uzbekistan at the invitation of the Ministry of Foreign Affairs and consulted with various officials in Tashkent. During the same trip he spent several days in Almaty at the invitation of the Kazakh Institute for Strategic Studies, including participation in a Kazakhstan–EU conference.

Although only the authors are responsible for the analyses and conclusions, they have been aided in their work by many others. In particular, Paul Stares, Director of Studies at the Japan Center for International Exchange in Tokyo, has provided assistance to Watanabe and more generally. Others consulted or otherwise assisting in the development of the report include:

Aziz Ait Said, *Senior Vice President for Russia/CIS, Total Fina, Paris*

Roy Allison, *Head, Russia and Eurasia Program, Royal Institute of International Affairs, London*

Aschot Amirdschanjan, *Foreign Political Editor, Free Radio, Berlin*

M. Ashimbayev, *Director, Kazakh Institute for Strategic Studies, Office of the President of the Republic of Kazakhstan*

Hüseyin Bagci, *Middle East Technical University, Ankara*

Piero Bassetti, *Chairman, Globus and Locus, Milan; Chairman of the Trilateral Commission Italian Group*

Boris Berezovsky, *Member of the State Duma, Moscow; former Executive Secretary of the CIS and Deputy Secretary of the Security Council of the Russian Federation (in charge of Caucasus/Chechnya), Moscow*

Gilles Bertrand, *Forward Studies Unit, European Commission, Brussels*

Boris Biancheri, *Chairman, Ansa, Rome; Chairman, ISPI, Milan*

Dieter Boden, *Special Envoy of the UN Secretary General in Georgia*

Clifford Bond, *Director, Office of Caucasus and Central Asian Affairs, U.S. Department of State, Washington, D.C.*

Jean-Marc Braichet, *International Dept. for Energy, Ministry of Energy, Paris*

Zbigniew Brzezinski, *Counsellor, Center for Strategic and International Studies, Washington, D.C.; former U.S. Assistant to the President for National Security Affairs*

Ewald Böhlke, *DaimlerChrysler, Berlin*

Umberto Cappuzzo, *Former Chief of Staff of the Italian Army, Rome*

Salvatore Carrubba, *Culture Alderman, Municipality of Milan; former Managing Editor, Il Sole 24 Ore, Milan*

Carey Cavanaugh, *Special Negotiator for S/NIS/RC, U.S. Department of State, Washington, D.C.*

Fausto Cereti, *Chairman, Alitalia, Rome*

Robert Corzine, *Energy Editor,* The Financial Times, *London*

Alexander Davydov, *Member, Analytical Department, Council of the Federation, Moscow*

Robert Donahue, *Editorial Pages Editor,* International Herald Tribune, *Paris*

Chris Donnelly, *Special Advisor on Eastern and Central Europe and the Former Soviet Union, NATO, Brussels*

Kamol Dusmetov, *Deputy Chairman, State Commission of Drug Control, Cabinet of Ministers of Uzbekistan, Tashkent*

Jonathan Elkind, *Director for Russia/Ukraine/Eurasia Affairs, U.S. National Security Council, Washington, D.C.*

Bill Emmott, *Editor,* The Economist, *London; Chairman of the Trilateral Commission British Group*

Jamila Fattah, *Caspian and Middle East Advisor, BP Amoco, London*

Martin Fenner, *Desk Officer for Central Asia, Foreign and Commonwealth Office, London*

Alain Frachon, *Editor-in-Chief,* Le Monde, *Paris*

Arndt Freytag von Loringhoven, *German Foreign Ministry*

Roland Galharague, *Deputy Director, Policy Planning Staff (CAP), Ministry of Foreign Affairs, Paris*

Rim Giniyatullin, *Director, International Agency for the Rescue of the Aral Sea, Tashkent*

Sergei Glasyev, *Chairman, Economics Committee, State Duma, Moscow*

Paul Goble, *Director of Communications, Radio Free Europe/Radio Liberty*

Thomas Graham, *Senior Associate, Carnegie Endowment for International Peace; former Head of the Political/Internal Unit and Acting Political Counselor at the U.S. Embassy in Moscow*

Brigitte Granville, *Royal Institute of International Affairs, London*

Vagif Guseynov, *Member of the Board of Directors, SISTEMA, Moscow*

Charles Heck, *North American Director, The Trilateral Commission*

Jeffrey Hertzfeld, *Senior Partner, Salans, Hertzfeld & Heilbronn, Paris*

Reinhard Hesse, *Advisor to the German Government on Islamic Affairs, Munich*

James E. Hogan, *Lawyer, Salans, Hertzfeld & Heilbronn, Paris*

Didier Houssin, *Director for Energy (DIMA), Ministry of Industry, Paris*

Karl Kaiser, *Otto-Wolff Director, Research Institute of the German Council on Foreign Relations (DGAP), Berlin*

Abduladid Kamilov, *National Center for the Control of Drugs, Cabinet of Ministers, Republic of Uzbekistan*

Robert P. Kaplan, *Director and former Chairman, Hurricane Hydrocarbons, Toronto; former Solicitor General of Canada; Honorary Consul in Canada for the Republic of Kazakhstan*

Sergei Karaganov, *Deputy Director, Institute of Europe, Russian Academy of Sciences; Chairman, Council on Defense and Foreign Policy*

O. Khalikov, *Administration for European Countries, Foreign Ministry of Uzbekistan*

Andrei Kokoshin, *Member of the State Duma, Moscow; Vice President of the Russian Academy of Sciences; former Secretary of the Russian Security Council*

George Kolt, *National Intelligence Officer for Russia and Eurasia, NIC, Washington, D.C.*

Terry Koonce, *President, ExxonMobil Production, Houston; former President, Exxon Ventures (CIS), Inc.*

Murat Laumulin, *Coordinator for Foreign Policy and Security Affairs of the Republic of Kazakhstan*

Véronique le Blanc, *International Secretariat, Defence Planning and Operations Divisions, NATO, Brussels*

Anne Leahy, *Diplomat-in-Residence, Centre for International and Security Studies, York University; former Ambassador of Canada to Russia*

Jeremy Lester, *DG1A, Human Rights and Democratization, European Commission, Brussels*

Michael Libal, *German Ambassador to Kazakhstan*

Anatol Lieven, *Editor,* Strategic Comments, *International Institute for Strategic Studies, London*

Nancy Lubin, *President, JNA Associates, Washington, D.C.*

Whitney MacMillan, *Former Chairman of the Board and Chief Executive Officer, Cargill, Inc., Minneapolis*

Patricia Manceau, *Directorate General for European Economic Affairs, Ministry of Foreign Affairs, Paris*

Fayaz Manji, *Program Manager for Central Asia, Aga Khan Foundation, Toronto*

M. Mashkamilov, *Department of Public Affairs, State Committee of the Republic of Uzbekistan for Border Control*

Anna Matveeva, *Royal Institute of International Affairs, London*

Barbara Minderjahn, *Cologne*

Gregory Mitchell, *Houston*

John Mitchell, *Royal Institute of International Affairs, London*

Aymeri de Montesquiou, *Member of the French Senate, Paris*

Damon C. Morris, *Assistant North American Director, The Trilateral Commission*

I. Mustafaev, *Deputy Minister of Foreign Affairs, Republic of Uzbekistan*

Klaus Naumann, *Former General Inspector of the German Bundeswehr and Chairman of NATO's Military Committee, Brussels*

Niels-Jorgen Nehring, *Director, Danish Institute of International Affairs (DUPI), Copenhagen*

Dan Nielsen, *Ambassador at the Royal Danish Ministry of Foreign Affairs, Copenhagen*

Vladimir Norov, *Ambassador of Uzbekistan to the Federal Republic of Germany, Berlin*

Makito Noda, *Chief Program Officer, Japan Center for International Exchange, Tokyo*

Lucio Noto, *Vice Chairman, ExxonMobil Corporation, Fairfax*

Martha Brill Olcott, *Senior Associate, Carnegie Endowment for International Peace, Washington, D.C.*

Roza Otunbayeva, *Ambassador of the Kyrgyz Republic to the United Kingdom, London*

Philipp Pachomov, *Unit for Russia and CIS Studies, Körber Foundation and German Council on Foreign Relations (DGAP), Berlin*

Wolfgang Pape, *Forward Studies Unit, European Commission, Brussels*

Evgeni Primakov, *Member of the State Duma, Moscow; former Russian Prime Minister*

Vladimir Putin, *President, Russian Federation, Moscow*

Leopold Radauer, *Director for Russia/NIS/Balkans, European Council, Brussels*

Jean Radvanyi, *Institut National des Langues et Civilisations Orientales (INALCO), Paris*

William Ramsay, *Deputy Executive Director in charge of CIS, International Energy Agency, Paris*

Odile Rémik-Adim, *Director, Central Asia Dept., Ministry of Foreign Affairs, Paris*

Paul Révay, *European Director, The Trilateral Commission, Paris*

Charles Richards, *Middle East Advisor, BP Amoco, London*

Dmitri Rogozin, *Chairman of the Committee for International Affairs, State Duma, Moscow*

John Roper, *Royal Institute of International Affairs, London*

Olivier Roy, *Researcher at FNSP/CERI and at CAP, Ministry of Foreign Affairs, Paris*

Eugene Rumer, *Visiting Fellow, Washington Institute for Near East Policy, Washington, D.C.; former Member of the Policy Planning Staff, U.S. Department of State*

Sabir Saidov, *Senior Advisor to the Minister of Foreign Affairs, Republic of Uzbekistan*

Rafik Saifulin, *Director, Institute for Strategic and Regional Studies, Office of the President of the Republic of Uzbekistan, Tashkent*

François Sauzey, *European Press Officer, The Trilateral Commission, Paris*

Ulrich Schöning, *Head of the OSCE Center in the Republic of Kazakhstan*

Stephen Sestanovich, *Ambassador-at-Large and Special Advisor to the U.S. Secretary of State on the New Independent States, Washington, D.C.*

Shi Ze, *Vice President, China Institute of International Studies, Beijing*

Hiroshi Shiojiri, *Director, New Independent States Division, European and Oceanic Affairs Bureau, Ministry of Foreign Affairs, Tokyo*

Umberto Silvestri, *Chairman, STET International, Rome*

Guillaume de Spoelberch, *Executive Director, Agha Khan Foundation, Brussels*

Miodrag Soric, *Editor-in-Chief, East European Service,* Deutsche Welle, *Cologne*

N. Srednii, *Department of Public Affairs, State Committee of the Republic of Uzbekistan for Border Control*

Helga Steeg, *Chairman, Transit Agreement of the Energy Charter Treaty; former Executive Director, International Energy Agency, Bonn*

Bulat Sultanov, *Department Head, Kazakh Institute for Strategic Studies, Office of the President of the Republic of Kazakhstan*

Timo Summa, *Director DG1A, CIS and TACIS, European Commission, Brussels*

Jean-Claude Thébault, *Director, Forward Studies Unit, European Commission, Brussels*

Anne de Tinguy, *Fondation Nationale des Sciences Politiques FNSP/CERI, Paris*

Frank Umbach, *German Council on Foreign Relations, Berlin*

Ibrahim Usmonov, *Chairman of International Affairs, Interethnic Relations and Culture Committee, Maglisi Oli (Parliament) of Tajikistan, Dushambe*

Tomohiko Uyama, *Associate Professor, Slavic Research Center, Hokkaido University, Sapporo*

Ernesto Vellano, *Secretary General of the Trilateral Commission Italian Group, Turin*

Dmitro Vydrin, *Director, European Institute for Integration and Development, Kiev*

Miki Wajima, *Researcher, Institute for Russian and East European Economic Studies, Tokyo*

Edward L. Warner, *U.S. Assistant Secretary of Defense for Strategy and Threat Reduction, Washington, D.C.*

Ed Webb, *Head, Central Asia and Transcaucasus Dept., Foreign and Commonwealth Office, London*

Cees Wittebrood, *Head of Unit, DG1A, NIS/Caucasus/Central Asia, European Commission, Brussels*

Enders Wimbush, *Vice President for International Strategy and Policy, Hicks & Associates, Washington, D.C.*

John Wolf, *Special Advisor to the President and Secretary of State for Caspian Basin Energy Diplomacy, U.S. Department of State, Washington, D.C.*

Grigori Yavlinsky, *Member of the State Duma, Moscow; Leader of the Yabloko Parliamentary Group; Chairman, Centre for Economic and Political Research, Moscow*

Yermukhamet Yertysbayev, *Director, Kazakhstan Institute for Strategic Studies, Almaty*

Bulat Yessekin, *Director, National Environmental Center for Sustainable Development, Republic of Kazakhstan*

Susumu Yoshida, *Senior Advisor for CIS, China, and Northeast Asia, Nissho Iwai Corporation, Tokyo*

Robert Zoellick, *Fellow, German Marshall Fund of the United States; former U.S. Under Secretary of State*

Gennedi Zyuganov, *Member of the State Duma, Moscow; Chairman, Russian Communist Party*

Table of Contents

List of Tables

I. Introduction

Though the states of Central Asia are known in Trilateral countries largely for their energy potential, they are in fact part of a thorough-going strategic transformation of Eurasia. This strategic transformation is most vividly seen in the fall of the USSR and the ongoing transformation of China, but it has a Central Asian dimension. It is the purpose of this report to describe this dimension and to show the strategic stakes Trilateral countries have in a stable outcome there.

However, at the outset, the authors must acknowledge a dilemma. We have chosen to focus primarily on the states of Central Asia (Kazakhstan, Kyrgyzstan, Tajikistan, Turkmenistan, and Uzbekistan). These states (see Map 2 in the set of maps after page 2) are thought of as a unified region largely because of their common Soviet past. But they are all in a state of flux, internally and in their external orientations. They are also increasingly seen as part of a larger whole—the Caspian Basin if viewed as potential energy producers, or Zbigniew Brzezinski's "Eurasian Balkans" if viewed as a source of instability.

We have also found it necessary at times in this report to range beyond our defined region and speak of Azerbaijan and, less frequently, of the other states of the Caucasus, Georgia, and Armenia. Russia, China, Iran, Turkey, and even India are involved as new economic, geopolitical, and security orientations take shape. Yet we believe the narrower focus of our report is justified because it is not about energy or conflicts alone but rather the region's increasing integration into the wider world, its potential for both stability and instability, and Trilateral interests in the better outcome.

The flow of oil and gas into the world market will create links across the Caspian Sea and common economic opportunities and problems for the entire Basin. However, we are struck by the vast differences between the states of Central Asia and those of the South Caucasus, differences that are more important than similarities when the focus is, as in this report, the broader political, economic, and security factors that produce a stable or unstable outcome.

We also believe that, while there is the chance of Balkan-like conflicts across a broad geographic range from eastern Turkey into Mongolia, it will be crucial to understand the root causes of particular conflicts. While common threads of state weakness, ethnic divisions and economic failure do exist, there are specific regional, country, and even local ingredients that must be understood. We think an appreciation of these unique factors is more likely to emerge from an examination of the "new" Central Asia and of the states within this region.

A. THE CONTEXT FOR TRILATERAL ENGAGEMENT

Successful Trilateral engagement in the new Central Asia depends upon understanding three interrelated sources of potential profit and peril: the dynamics of a complex and changing region, the increased engagement in the region of neighboring large powers, and energy development.

1. Challenges from a Complex and Changing Region
The Russian historian, Sergey Soloviev, once complained that, for much of Eurasia, nature was less a mother than a "stepmother," hiding whatever riches were given under harsh climatic extremes. Central Asia knows these extremes, from waterless, scorching deserts to high mountain plateaus. Large areas east of the Caspian Sea, across the steppes of Kazakhstan and the deserts of Turkmenistan and Uzbekistan, are uninhabited or sparsely populated (see Map 1 in the set of maps after this page). The great urban civilizations of the region grew up around the oases and the watercourses that once formed part of the Great Silk Route linking China with the Mediterranean. The bands of populated areas still stretch along two rivers—the Amu Darya and Syr Darya—that flow toward the Aral Sea. The most heavily populated areas in Central Asia are far from the Caspian Sea. Tashkent, the capital of Uzbekistan, has a population of about 4 million. The fertile, well-watered Ferghana Valley not far southeast of Tashkent has some 10 million inhabitants, divided between Tajikistan, Kyrgyzstan, and Uzbekistan.

The region has inherited a sub-standard transportation network, the result of both natural conditions and long-term neglect. Often the best connections between two parts of one state are through another. The road and rail links were built by Tsarist or Soviet engineers who never imagined that internal administrative boundaries would become international ones. Rail and air links aimed to tie the region to Moscow, not to encourage regional integration or links to neighboring areas outside the empire. The prospects of oil and gas development and foreign assistance have decisively improved direct air links between the capital cities of Azerbaijan, Kazakhstan, and Uzbekistan and major outside capitals.

Historically, the states of Central Asia have been shaped in succession by Islam, the great Mongol invasion, isolation, Russian imperialism, and Sovietization. The great Silk Road cities, such as Bukhara and Samarkand, were integral parts of the Islamic world well before the coming of the Mongols in the 13th century. Outside the great urban centers, nomads wandered the steppe and desert regions. The Portuguese discovery of the sea route from Europe to China led to the decline of the Silk Road and the region's isolation and decline. Russian imperial encroachment into the northern Kazakh steppes already in the 18th century and into the rest of the region in the 19th brought new political and economic subordination.

The reconquest of the region by the Soviets brought increased development, as well as new administrative divisions outlining the Union Republics that are now the independent states of Kazakhstan, Kyrgyzstan, Tajikistan, Turkmenistan, and Uzbekistan. The separate Soviet administrative districts provided not only the boundaries for the new states but a nascent and subordinate administrative apparatus that turned out to be a key supporting structure for independence. The Union Republics of the Soviet era also gave an organizational, cultural, and political boost to the Kazakhs, Kyrgyz, Tajiks, Turkmen, and Uzbeks. The land area and population of the five new states are presented in Table I-1.

Of course, the Soviet purpose was not to create new nations but to manage a multinational empire. Moscow wanted to deepen divisions in this Islamic region. Along with giving titular nationalities a boost in their respective republics, Soviet authorities drew borders designed to leave significant minority populations stranded in each republic. They divided in order to rule. Thus, at the time of the breakup of the Soviet Union, nearly 30 percent of the residents of Uzbekistan were not ethnic Uzbeks, while ethnic Uzbeks comprised a quarter of the population of Tajikistan (see pie charts alongside Map 1). With the large concentration of Russians in Northern Kazakhstan—over 6 million—the Russian and Kazakh populations were nearly equal, though Kazakhstan claims that ethnic Kazakhs are now an absolute majority. The Ferghana Valley is an especially complex area. It was divided between Tajikistan, Uzbekistan, and Kyrgyzstan, with each portion containing significant numbers of at least one other nationality (e.g., 14 percent of the population in the Kyrgyz portion of

TABLE I-1
The New States of Central Asia: Land Area and Population

	Land Area (sq km)	Population (thousands, 1999)
Kazakhstan	2,724,900	15,491
Kyrgyzstan	199,900	4,732
Tajikistan	143,100	6,188
Turkmenistan	491,200	4,993
Uzbekistan	447,400	22,231
Total	4,006,500	53,635

Source: Interstate Statistical Committee of the Commonwealth of Independent States, www.unece.org/stats/cisstat/maco0.htm.

the Ferghana are Uzbeks, rising to 28 percent in the urban center of Osh). Riots between Kyrgyz and Uzbeks in Osh over housing in 1990 led to hundreds of deaths. These riots provided for many observers the model of what could—and for some, almost surely would—go wrong in these new states.

The potential significance of this patchwork ethnic distribution extends beyond the new Central Asia into neighboring states. As Map 1 indicates, there are large numbers of Uzbeks and Tajiks and Turkmen in Afghanistan and an important presence of Kazakhs and Kyrgyz in China. (There are also more Azeris in Iran than in Azerbaijan.) The Kazakhs, Kyrgyz, Turkmen, and Uzbeks (and Azeris) are Turkic peoples; the Tajiks speak an Indo-European language related to Farsi spoken in Iran.

Islam is a major factor in the mix. Central Asian states are part of a world Islamic civilization, though in the past these links have been weakened, suppressed, and managed by Moscow. Trilateral countries, Russia, and China are of course concerned with radical Islamic movements which might arise in one or more Central Asian states. Like the Taliban in Afghanistan, a fundamentalist regime in Central Asia would become a source of drugs, terrorism, and regional instability. But the fear of Islamic radicalism should not obscure the central importance of Islamic culture to the stabilizing of these countries. The growth of civil society will ultimately depend on the emergence and flourishing of mainstream and moderate Islamic forces, which Trilateral states should support and encourage.

The lens of basic economic and social indicators gives a picture of considerable distress in what were already the poorest areas of the old Soviet Union. Table I-2 gives output figures for the countries of Central Asia for 1993, 1995, and 1997, relative to 1991. Output held up better in Uzbekistan than in any other country. Tajikistan, suffering through civil war, had the sharpest fall to 1997, to 32 percent of the 1991 level. Life expectancy has fallen during the 1990s in Kyrgyzstan and Tajikistan. Infant mortality has risen in Kazakhstan. The number of physicians per 100,000 has dropped in all of the countries but Turkmenistan, dropping by nearly 20 percent in war-torn Tajikistan. Nearly universal literacy rates are falling, especially in the region's rural areas, as schools close or receive inadequate government support. Basic social infrastructure, from hospitals to schools and universities are coming under increasing stress. These strains in the economic and social fabric are a potential source for failed states in the coming decade.

TABLE I-2
Central Asian Economies: Declining Output after 1991
(1991 = 100)

	1993	1995	1997
Kazakhstan	85	68	70
Kyrgyzstan	73	55	62
Tajikistan	63	44	32
Turkmenistan	85	64	47
Uzbekistan	87	83	86

Source: Günther Taube and Jeromin Zettelmeyer, "Output Decline and Recovery in Uzbekistan: Past Performance and Future Prospects," IMF Working Paper 98/132 (September, 1998): 4.

Independence has brought profound changes to trade patterns, most markedly a relative decline of trade with Russia. The biggest beneficiaries, though, have not been other Central Asian states but outside trading partners, including Trilateral states and China. As might be expected, foreign direct investment has been low, especially outside the energy sector (see Table I-3).

In the past decade, an increasing number of analysts inside and outside the region have ceased to question whether the new states of Central Asia will survive. Instead, these analysts assume their persistence and turn instead to the pressing question of what kind of states they will be. The most troubling answer is that these will be

TABLE I-3
Foreign Direct Investment in Central Asia
(US$ million)

	1996	1997	1989–97
Kazakhstan	1,100	1,200	4,267
Kyrgyzstan	46	50	247
Tajikistan	20	20	86
Turkmenistan	129	108	652
Uzbekistan	50	60	216

Source: United Nations Department of Economic and Social Affairs, *World Economic and Social Survey, 1998* (New York: United Nations, 1998), 31, cited in Neil MacFarlane, *Western Engagement in the Caucasus and Central Asia* (London: Royal Institute of International Affairs, 1999), 42.

weak states, which under stress could become failing ones. Tajikistan has been on the edge of this abyss, as has Georgia across the Caspian. Afghanistan is already the regional model for such a negative outcome. The great hope or fear of the early and mid-1990s that a resurgent Russia would swallow these states has given way to the realization that no state in or outside the region is in the position to manage a serious and sustained crisis there.

The characteristics of weak states are ineffective institutions, authoritarian regimes, and corruption. In the region, only Kyrgyzstan can be called truly committed to democratic institutions and pluralism. Though not without problems of internal corruption, crime, and weak social services, Kyrgyzstan has managed to create the only state in the region where basic laws are fair and relatively transparent, discussion is free, and economic risk predictable. Turkmenistan, Uzbekistan, and Kazakhstan are dominated by strong and authoritarian-minded presidents; though Turkmenistan is a full-fledged police state and Kazakhstan is not, with Uzbekistan in between. Soviet-style elections are in fashion here and across the Caspian in Azerbaijan. Strong rulers warn of Islamic fundamentalism and prefer order to human rights. The leadership defends its preferences as the key to economic and social recovery, yet a strong hand at the top has so far not brought prosperity or stemmed the decline in basic social services. Corruption is eating away at the heart of the ruling elite, making the state appear strong in police functions but nearly invisible as a provider of basic social services. An additional source of instability is the fact that these regimes are over-personalized. They will in fact be sorely tested as the great leaders—some in frail health and in their seventies—pass from the scene and succession struggles emerge.

Trilateral policymakers need to remember that weak states, economies, and societies are breeding grounds for ethnic and religious conflict, nationalism and Islamic radicalism, drug trafficking, and a wide variety of social ills. Moreover, it is vital to remember that internal weakness and decay in one or more states of the region now arises in the context of the breakdown of the region's former isolation. Though none of these states is next door to Trilateral countries, problems there will simply be more difficult to contain. They will spill over into Russia, China, and other adjacent states of importance, ultimately posing challenges to Trilateral interests as well.

2. Regional Powers: The Changing Eurasian Context

Eurasia is in the midst of a strategic transformation, and the new Central Asia is part of it. Moscow, the once powerful center of Eurasia, has become weak and distracted by its internal challenges; new states like those in Central Asia have emerged; and major states of the Eurasian rim, such as China and India, exhibit a dynamism now absent from the heartland's old center. For decades, Moscow exerted continuous pressure of one sort or another on the outer rim, but it now appears that the pattern has changed. A more dynamic rim has begun to influence the states at the center.

President Putin has, of course, radically altered the image and substance of Russian leadership. Yet this new dynamism has yet to transform the economic, political, and military foundations of power that will ultimately determine whether Russia has a strong hand to play in the region. Putin has to date played a more skillful hand in the region, recognizing the destructive results for Russian influence of the combination of old-fashioned imperial demands and new-fangled Russian weakness. Yet, even with Putin, Russia remains a declining power in the region and is widely seen as such by the leaders of the region.

The remarkable "reversal of polarity" in Eurasia driven by Russia's decline from the role of regional hegemon is the new context for Trilateral engagement. New patterns of diplomatic interaction have arisen. Economic dynamism in China, India, and elsewhere in Asia is shifting patterns of energy consumption and creating new trade links. The proliferation of advanced military technology, particularly ballistic and cruise missiles and weapons of mass destruction, is creating a new military context in Eurasia, especially in the Persian Gulf and in South and East Asia.

In Central Asia these trends are less dramatic but present nonetheless. The states of the region have small populations and have suffered a decade of slow growth or outright economic decline. Their militaries are modest; Soviet hand-me-down equipment predominates. Only Uzbekistan has made a serious attempt to create even modest projection capability. But the Central Asian states are finally actors in their own right. They have potentially conflicting interests in their own region. Long-term Uzbek–Kazakh rivalry, for example, is a major and potentially unsettling dynamic within Central Asia. Central Asian states are influenced by neighboring lands and see their own interests engaged there. They have all fashioned "multi-vectored" foreign policies—the term is a Russian one—which seek to develop new ties with Moscow, Beijing, Tehran, New Dehli, and the Trilateral countries. Their very vulnerability inclines them to broaden their circle of friends and partners. Moreover, they cannot pursue their newly defined national interests on their own. They need the cooperation of others inside and outside the region, creating potential sources of competition and rivalry within Central Asia and outside it.

Central Asia borders some of the most important states in the new Eurasia: a weakened Russia, an emerging China, and a changing Iran. Turkey and the countries of a nuclear South Asia are, in the geopolitical sense, nearby. There is a Central Asian dimension in the strategic thinking of these neighboring states, one frequently neglected in Trilateral analysis. Major sources of conflict, such as Afghanistan or the various conflicts in the Caucasus, influence the region. Every Central Asia leader saw chaos in Tajikistan as a continuation of the struggle in Afghanistan, and thus as a potential source of instability for the rest of Central Asia. Prospects for economic gain, the fear of instability, and the emerging competition among neighbors draw outside actors to Central Asia. Even as the players and stakes of the game mutliply, the rules are far from clear and the local and regional institutions to manage this growing interaction and competition are less developed. Assumptions about the interests of other parties are untested, and the threshold for the use of force is presumed low, much lower at any rate than in Europe or East Asia.

In this context, it is important to understand the interests and perceptions of the key outside actors, particularly Russia, China, and Iran. Russia has been since Tsarist times the dominating force in Central Asia. It is the power that has had to adjust the most to the independence of the region's states, for that very independence is a sign of declining influence. Throughout much of the 1990s, Russia sought to stem its loss of influence there through the creation of an integrated political, economic, and security community—the Commonwealth of Independent States (CIS). Central Asian states have been among the most enthusiastic in supporting the CIS, especially in the beginning. In 1994 President Nazarbayev of Kazakhstan in fact floated his own version of a Euro-Asian Union.

Russia has also been involved from the very beginning of the post-Soviet period in armed conflicts in and around the region. It now maintains stationed military forces only in Tajikistan, though it has a series of bilateral agreements with other states that give it access to strategic sites and transit rights, and that establish a range of cooperative programs with regional militaries and border guards. Yet it is obvious that Russia's declining military capability, its distractions in Chechnya, and local interests in maintaining control over key security institutions have created in the past several years an accelerating decline of Russia's military presence and influence in the region. That decline includes the collapse of the Tashkent Collective Security Treaty, with Uzbekistan, Georgia, and Kazakhstan formally withdrawing from what was already an admittedly moribund collective security regime. Russian border guards are being phased out in Kyrgyzstan. Russia's forces—regular military and border guards—in Tajikistan have become largely indigenized at the lower ranks, with ethnic Tajiks flocking to Russian service for the better pay and provisions ethnic Russians want no part of.

Russia's economic influence in the region remains important, chiefly because of Soviet-era connections among Russian and local elites and the continued importance of local Russians in various sectors of the economy. China has become in several states a leading supplier of consumer goods. Non-Russian energy and mining companies, including from China, dominate the big projects in Kazakhstan, Turkmenistan, Azerbaijan, and Uzbekistan. Attempts to create CIS or special free trade and customs zones have not stemmed the shift away from trade with Russia or other CIS partners toward the outside world.

Beyond the practical issues of security and economics, Russia's self-definition is in some sense tied to the role it carves out in the former Soviet Union in general and in Central Asia in particular. Old imperial attitudes and temptations remain in some quarters of the Russian foreign policy community. Even if President Putin embraces a more realistic and modernized definition of Russian interests, freeing Russia from the trap of seeing each and every development in the region as potentially a matter of vital interests, Russia can never be indifferent to developments there. Russia's own security and internal development would still be influenced by the fate of its neighbors, particularly if that fate included state collapse, ethnic violence, and regional conflicts that could spill over into Russia itself. Russia is thus a key continuing player in the region, though no longer in the driver's seat.

Russia's declining fortunes affect China. In the near term, China would like to see Russia remain a guarantor of stability in Central Asia, even as Moscow cedes its position in the local economies to China. However, in the long run, China wants to establish its own levers of influence in the region. Several key elements of the Russian–Chinese strategic partnership focus on Central Asia, including agreements with three Central Asia countries on transparency and demilitarization along the old Sino-Soviet border there. Russia, China, Tajikistan, Kazakhstan, and Kyrgyzstan have created a regular summit meeting of the five state leaders (in which the President of Uzbekistan participated as an observer in 2000).

China has become a major trading partner for Kazakhstan, Kyrgyzstan, and Uzbekistan. However, Beijing's strategic interests in the region arise from its own concern for stability in Xinjiang, a region with a large Muslim minority population. Beijing does not want to see weak states in Central Asia become havens for its own Muslim separatists or to have instability in Central Asia spill over into northwest China. It wants to see, at least in the short term, Russia continue to provide a security blanket for the new states. However, Chinese strategic analysts see the growing weakness of Russia in Central Asia and know Beijing must be prepared to act if chaos emerges there.

The shifting fortunes of Russia and China in the region are thus a medium- and long-term issue of some importance for stability in Central Asia. Though some Trilateral analysts see Russian–Chinese strategic cooperation as detrimental, at least in Central Asia it is creating a basis for managing what could well be a very uncertain future. Russian–Chinese strategic cooperation might be a building block of regional cooperation. Trilateral countries have an interest in encouraging this kind of cooperation in the region and perhaps broadening it to create a mechanism for increased Trilateral–regional dialogue.

Like China, Iran has been content to date to support Russia's role as security guarantor—both in Tajikistan and in the Caucasus. Tehran sees a greater near-term danger from unpredictability in the new states and the outright challenge of Taliban-ruled Afghanistan than it does from traditional Russian imperialist ambitions in and around Iran. Islamic militant groups do support like-minded groups inside the former USSR, but Tehran has been very careful to avoid in Central Asia the kind of state-sponsored Islamic radicalism that it pursues in the Middle East.

Iranian and Russian views have overlapped in the dispute over the legal status of the Caspian Sea and its energy resources. Like Russia, Iran sees little it can do about efforts by Azerbaijan and Kazakhstan to move ahead with national energy projects in nearby offshore areas. However, also like Russia, Iran sees the importance of becoming a larger player in the energy sector in the area. Iran has negotiated energy swaps with Turkmenistan and supported the opening of rail and other transportation links between the two states. Tehran clearly wants a larger role in energy development in the region, one that could more easily emerge if U.S.–Iranian rapprochement gathers momentum. The coming to power of reform-minded President Khatami and the success of his supporters in recent elections may eventually make possible improvements in U.S.–Iranian relations, something that would certainly give Iran's role in Central Asia a boost.

Turkey, India, and Pakistan each have an increasing presence in one or more states of the region, foreshadowing what will eventually be a much wider pattern of interaction between Central Asia and key states of the Eurasian rimland. Turkey especially got off to a fast start in the region and continues to be the sponsor of the "Turkic Summit," a yearly gathering of leaders from Turkey, Azerbaijan, Turkmenistan, Kyrgyzstan, Kazakhstan, and Uzbekistan. Turkey's influence on the west side of the Caspian, in Azerbaijan and Georgia, is of unquestioned importance, but it is not as important a player as it would like to be to the east of the Caspian. Early evocations of common Turkic linguistic and cultural bonds were not enough to sustain relationships that required large amounts of trade, assistance, and strategic cooperation. Pakistani strategic analysts see Central Asia as expanded "strategic depth," though there is little apparent enthusiasm in Central Asia for taking sides in South Asia. India is not content merely to frustrate Pakistani ambitions in the region. It sees itself as an emerging major power and thus wants to increase its influence in Central Asia.

This growing interaction with Eurasian rim states will take place on a largely unregulated field, absent substantial efforts to create acceptable regional institutions and rules of the road. Trilateral countries have given little thought to what they see as this "backside"of Russia or China, yet it remains a potentially important theater in the geopolitical transformation of Eurasia. Helping guide this transformation to a stable outcome is a matter of Trilateral interest. The vital interests of Trilateral states elsewhere in Eurasia and the growing interconnection of the new Central Asia with the wider world create an important set of "derivative interests" in the region. These derivative interests suggest a Trilateral role in encouraging dialogue among the major players, supporting the resolution of regional conflicts, and urging the establishment of rules of the road and institutional frameworks that would soften regional rivalries.

3. Energy Development

The economic future of Central Asia indeed depends in no small measure on the successful development of regional energy resources, concentrated in the Caspian Basin. The scale, pace, and pattern of development of these resources will be determined by a multitude of factors.

Especially in the early stages, there need to be large discoveries that can be developed and brought to markets at a reasonable cost. Large fields justify investment in the infrastructure needed for exploration, development, and export—infrastructure which can then be helpful in connection with other fields over time.

The giant Tengiz field in Kazakhstan, onshore near the Caspian Sea, was the largest oil field discovered in the world since the 1970s. Proven reserves at Tengiz are estimated between 6 and 9 billion barrels. Chevron, the lead international company involved, began negotiating with the old Soviet Union about the field in 1990. Tengizchevroil (TCO), a 50–50 joint venture between Chevron and Kazakh state-owned oil interests, came into being in 1993 and projected an investment of $20 billion over 40 years of production from the field. Later the TCO partnership was broadened. Mobil (now ExxonMobil) took up a 25 percent share (half of the Kazakh share). Russian interests were included as LukArco took up a 5 percent share (from Chevron).

The other large project that began around the same time is in the offshore Chirag, Azeri, and Guneshli (ACG) fields belonging to Azerbaijan. A broad consortium of international companies and SOCAR (State Oil Company of Azerbaijan) signed this project deal in 1994 and created the Azerbaijani International Operating Company (AIOC) to run the project. Estimates at the time were for capital investments of $8 billion and production of nearly 4 billion barrels of oil over 30 years. Russian interests (Lukoil holds a 10 percent share) were included in the consortium from the beginning. The largest international shares went to BP and Amoco, now merged into a single company and serving as the operator for the consortium.

Two other very large discoveries have been made recently. In 2000 results are coming in from the first test drilling into the promising Kashagan formation in Kazakhstan's portion of the North Caspian Sea. Most participants are not providing reserve estimates until further test drilling is done, but the general sense seems to be that this field is as large or larger than Tengiz. The range of companies involved—with shares in OKIOC (Offshore Kazakhstan International Operating Company)—is again broad, but so far does not include Russian interests. The other recent very large discovery is of gas in Azerbaijan's offshore Shakh–Deniz field, with AIOC (thus BP Amoco) as the operator.

Estimates of the overall reserves of the Caspian Basin and of the scale of future oil and gas production have varied widely over the past decade or so. As estimates emerged in the early nineties that were far larger than Soviet-era estimates, some touted the Caspian Basin as a potential "second Persian Gulf." Subsequent estimates greatly moderated expectations. The Kashagan and Shakh–Deniz discoveries may raise estimates somewhat, but the more common comparison is likely to remain a "new North Sea." There is much exploration still to be undertaken. As of early 1998, there were "roughly 260 undrilled promising petroleum-bearing geological formations in the Caspian area," according to an industry leader.[1]

The largest oil reserves are in Kazakhstan. The largest gas reserves are in Turkmenistan. Azerbaijan, across the Caspian Sea, is the third member of the Caspian energy troika. Tables I-4 and I-5, from a recent study, present oil and gas "production potential" profiles for the Caspian region from 1990 to 2020. These "unrisked" profiles produce overly optimistic numbers, but give some idea of expected relative production over time from four countries. Kazakhstan remains the largest oil producer throughout the period (with about 60 percent of its production from the Tengiz, Kashagan, and Karachaganak projects), and Turkmenistan the largest gas producer. The largest proportional increases in both oil and gas production are in Kazakhstan and then Azerbaijan.

Production rises to about 4 million barrels per day in 2020 in the "unrisked" oil profile, about three times expected production in 2000. In the "risked" profile in the same recent study, oil production peaks

TABLE I-4
Oil Production Potential
(thousands of barrels per day)

	1990	1995	2000	2005	2010	2015	2020
Kazahkstan	516	409	716	1,390	1,684	2,186	2,531
Azerbaijan	251	186	290	530	1,285	1,320	1,093
Turkmenistan	114	97	146	239	307	304	251
Uzbekistan	68	169	172	159	118	107	97
Caspian Total	949	861	1,324	2,318	3,394	3,917	3,972

Source: Hilary McCutcheon and Richard Olson, "Risk Management, Financing Availability Keys to Winning in Caspian Region," *Oil & Gas Journal*, 24 July 2000, Table 1.

at about 2.4 million barrels per day in 2015, about twice expected 2000 production. This study analyzed 32 key projects (including three pipeline projects) and estimated, in the "unrisked" profile, that the average cost of bringing 18 billion barrels of oil to market over 30 years would be about $10 per barrel (including capital expenditures, operating expenses, and transportation). In the "risked" profile, the average cost is also about $10 per barrel over these 30 years.[2]

These cost estimates remind us that the market outlook beyond the Caspian region will be vital in determining the course of Caspian oil and gas development. Spot oil prices have increased dramatically in the period during which the authors of the current report have been at work. At the beginning of 1999, the benchmark price of North Sea Brent was under $11 per barrel. As the finishing touches are put on this report in September 2000, the same benchmark price is over $32 per barrel. The outlook for various Caspian region oil projects would be very different with an oil price outlook in the $25–30 range rather than the $12–15 range. Gas markets work rather differently than oil markets. Gas is more complicated to transport, and sales are far more dependent on long-term contracts between particular sellers and particular buyers. There may already be more proven gas reserves in the Caspian region than markets can absorb in the short and medium term. But higher gas prices would tend to elicit higher gas production over time. Caspian gas is of greater commercial interest than oil for Europe over time. The largest part of incremental increases in global demand for both oil and gas in the next couple of decades is expected to come from East Asia.

TABLE I-5
Gas Production Potential
(millions of cubic feet per day)

	1990	1995	2000	2005	2010	2015	2020
Turkeminstan	8,491	2,960	4,286	6,190	8,515	10,839	12,732
Uzbekistan	3,935	4,607	5,253	5,745	5,813	6,109	6,421
Kazakhstan	643	434	1,009	1,917	3,457	5,039	5,729
Azerbaijan	969	643	606	1,027	3,114	3,813	3,973
Caspian Total	14,029	8,644	11,154	11,154	20,899	25,800	28,855

Source: Hilary McCutcheon and Richard Olson, "Risk management, Financing Availability Keys to Winning in Caspian Region," *Oil & Gas Journal*, 24 July 2000, Table 2.

Aside from these global factors, there are many regional and local factors that will affect the scale, pace, and pattern of energy development in the Caspian Basin. Some of these are technical factors, such as the differences between the North Caspian and South Caspian:

The northern and southern regions of the Caspian are different geologically. In the north, water depth over prospective structures is as shallow as two meters....The most northern portion of the Caspian Sea is typically ice-covered for 4–5 months a year. In the south, water depth ranges as great as 800 meters over prospective structures. Ice is not a factor, but storm-driven wave heights will be a concern, as will seismic activity and mud volcanoes. As a result, development in the two areas will look very different necessitating industrial infrastructure specialized to one area or the other. The north could be characterized by numerous smaller ice-resistant structures constructed and supported by a specialized shallow water fleet. In the south, development could tend toward very large deep-water structures with a significant number of subsea wells.[3]

The landlocked nature of the Caspian, and the political complexity of the wider area in which it sits, make more difficult the development of the needed exploration and production infrastructure.

Since the Caspian is land-locked, it does not have access to the worldwide resources of the oil and gas industry, such as marine drilling and construction fleets, or fabrication facilities. The Caspian region must be more self-sufficient than most developing hydrocarbon basins. Access is limited by either the Volga-Don Canal system or by overland routes. It will be necessary to develop the basic infrastructure to build and install production facilities.[4]

The landlocked nature of the Caspian and the political complexity of the wider area in which it sits also make more difficult, of course, the delivery of Caspian oil and gas to world markets. It is around the issue of pipelines that the politics of Caspian oil and gas have been particularly evident (see Map 3 in the set of maps after page 2).

In the days of the Soviet Union, the pipeline system, limited as it was, led into Russia. After the collapse of the Soviet Union,

> Chevron was the first company to embark on trying to build a pipeline in the Caspian region. When Chevron signed its contract for Tengiz in April 1993, it correctly identified the Russian route for oil exports as the most commercially expedient for its crude.[5]

A Caspian Pipeline Consortium (CPC) was formed—including a number of Europe- or U.S.-based firms along with Russian, Kazakh, and Omani state companies—to build a major pipeline from the Tengiz field to the Russian port of Novorossiysk on the Black Sea. The Russians in particular created many difficulties in the early years of the CPC, and the operators of the Tengiz field came up with creative alternative ways to export limited amounts of oil. In recent years, Russia has been more cooperative and it now appears this pipeline will be completed for use by June 2001. The initial capacity will be 560,000 barrels per day. "In step with expansions at the Tengiz concession, Chevron is committed to carry out further expansions on the CPC pipeline, which could eventually reach a capacity of 1.3 million barrels per day."[6]

We have noted that the other large project beginning at about the same time as Tengiz was the AIOC offshore Azeri–Chirag–Guneshli project. For export of AIOC's "early oil" work was undertaken on a pipeline from Baku to the Georgian Black Sea port of Supsa, a line making use of some existing pipe. Baku–Supsa was completed in December 1998. "Supsa is currently transporting all of AIOC's 105,000 barrels per day of production and could carry up to 150,000."[7]

The other existing route from Baku is north through Russia to the Black Sea. The long-standing pipeline on this northern route went through Chechnya, a line disrupted in the second Chechnya war. In April 2000, the Russian pipeline company Transneft announced that it had completed a new northern route that bypasses Chechnya. It proceeds north from Baku along the Caspian coastline through Dagestan. SOCAR has committed to shipping about 100,000 barrels per day of its own oil through this northern route.

There are commercially attractive export possibilities to Iran. There are four refineries in the northern part of Iran with a total capacity of 810,000 barrels per day.

These refineries are currently supplied with oil that is shipped from the south of the country. Iran would like to buy or sway Caspian crudes into these refineries and save the cost of shipping its oil north.

Iran has proposed to the Azeris that they sell 220,000 barrels per day under a long-term contract to its refineries. Iran would buy the oil outright from the Azeris for its Tabriz and Tehran refineries....The oil would be delivered through a new oil pipeline Iran has looked at building from Baku to Tabriz....

Kazakhstan and Turkmenistan, with their oil potential centered along the eastern shore of the Caspian, see the economics of a pipeline straight down to Iran as their most cost-effective solution.[8]

The U.S. government's sanctions against Iran prevent the participation of U.S. companies in such projects with Iran, but non-U.S. companies are moving forward to some extent—and all could move forward more quickly if and when U.S. sanctions are lifted.

The U.S. government has strongly supported a major proposed pipeline (with a capacity of about 1 million barrels per day) from Baku through Georgia to the Turkish Mediterranean port of Ceyhan. The U.S. government argues that this is a secure export route, passing through neither Russia nor Iran. Compared to routes to Black Sea ports, Baku–Ceyhan obviates the need for increased tanker traffic through the Bosporus (which Turkey strongly opposes). Intergovernmental agreements preparing the way for Baku–Ceyhan were signed with great fanfare at the OSCE summit in Istanbul in November 1999, and President Clinton has described the proposed line as of historic importance.

But it is not clear that Baku–Ceyhan is commercially viable, particularly if sanctions against Iran are lifted in the coming years (it will take several years for Baku–Ceyhan actually to be built). Even if sanctions against Iran are not lifted, given the other pipelines noted above, where will sufficient oil production come from to make Baku–Ceyhan commercially viable? Many in the industry complain that "as the U.S. government continues to pursue this geostrategic agenda, commercial considerations have become secondary and companies are being asked to shoulder the financial burden of paying for it."[9] The prospects for Baku–Ceyhan will improve if oil prices remain high, accelerating development in Azerbaijani fields, and if the Kashagan formation in Kazakhstan turns out to be a giant field from which some production is shipped through Baku.

The U.S. government has given related support to a Trans-Caspian Gas Pipeline (TCGP) from Turkmenistan across the Caspian Sea through Azerbaijan and Georgia to Turkey, the primary market for new gas contracts in the medium term. The alternative major pipelines for transporting Turkmenistan's gas to Turkey (and beyond) are through Russia and Iran.

Prospects for the TCGP have dimmed in recent months. The discovery of very large amounts of gas in the Shakh–Deniz offshore area not far from Baku has turned attention to feeding a gas pipeline through Azerbaijan and Georgia to Turkey from Shakh–Deniz.[10] Relations have cooled between Washington and Ashgabat. A key TCGP partner appears to be backing away from the project.[11] Moreover, Russia seems set to win the race to supply gas to the Turkish market. Russia's Gazprom together with Italy's ENI have begun construction (Italian and Japanese financing was announced early this year) of the "Blue Stream" gas pipeline under the Black Sea to Turkey. The Russian National Security Council has put construction of the "Blue Stream" at the top of its list of priorities. If, with U.S. assistance, Turkmenistan or Azerbaijan beat Russia in the competition for deliveries of gas to Turkey, Moscow may lose a project urgently needed for its own gas industry, which will remain an important part of the backbone of the Russian economy for a long time to come.

We noted above that the largest portion of incremental increases in demand in coming years are expected to come from Asia, and there are longer-term prospects for pipelines from Central Asia to the east. The strongest prospect is for a gas pipeline from Turkmenistan, particularly if China builds a gas pipeline from its coast to the Tarim Basin in western China, a pipeline to which the pipeline from Turkmenistan might then be attached. Prospects are weaker for an oil pipeline through Kazakhstan from the Caspian to China. A few years ago a Unocal-led consortium worked on the idea of a gas pipeline from Turkmenistan south through Afghanistan to markets in Pakistan and beyond, but the turbulence in Afghanistan has brought planning to a halt.

Trilateral interests in the secure flow of Caspian energy into the global market are clear. It is in the long-term best interest of both regional energy producers and the Trilateral states to encourage multiple pipelines. At the same time the pattern and sequence of multiple pipelines will need to be commercially as well as politically viable.

It is in the interests of Trilateral states to find ways to encourage the participation of Russian, Chinese, and even Iranian energy companies in the Caspian mix. Creating large, multinational coalitions of companies is a prudent political step, as well as a sound economic one. These coalitions encourage relevant parties to see the pipeline issue as a "win-win" prospect, not a "zero-sum" competition.

Encouraging the emergence of players with this outlook in Russia and other key neighboring states is a key to breaking the cycle of suspicion and sabotage of the energy ambitions of Caspian states and Trilateral companies.

One further issue is central. The challenge for the energy states of the region is not simply to earn revenue from energy exports but also to use that wealth to create the foundations for broad-based long-term economic growth and to address looming social problems. The potential distortions associated with a great increase in energy revenues are a danger to any state, but would further distort already troubled indigenous economic development in Central Asia. In addition, the fragile social fabric in these new states would be further weakened by the influx of great riches that go only to presidential palaces, monuments to great leaders, corruption, and elite enrichment. Given the uncertainty that hangs over the political regimes and societies in the new Central Asia, Trilateral energy companies, governments, and international financial institutions have to consider ways to encourage the productive use of oil wealth. The best place to start is to use the powerful carrots and sticks available to Trilateral and international institutions to encourage privatization and restructuring throughout the local economies. The often-neglected agricultural sector deserves major attention in this regard, and could open the way for economic progress for rural populations largely bypassed by oil and gas development.

B. CHALLENGES FOR TRILATERAL COUNTRIES

The most important challenge for Trilateral countries is understanding the role they could play in the new Central Asia's search for stability. No Trilateral country has defined this region as one of vital interests, but derivative Trilateral interests (e.g., in energy, moderate Islam, terrorism, drug trafficking, Russia, China, Iran) are significant. Moreover, the absence of vital interests gives Trilateral countries the possibility of creating a "win-win" engagement in the region, modeled on the cooperative, multinational yet highly competitive efforts of energy companies. Specifically, Trilateral countries have to address the challenges presented by the key factors outlined above. Policies so structured would aim at the following:

• strengthening the independence and viability of the new states;

- helping them enter the world economy;
- addressing serious humanitarian, social, and ecological problems;
- promoting the development of a strong oil and gas sector, in a manner supportive of broad economic and social progress;
- supporting multiple pipelines as a way of ensuring the smooth flow of energy from the region;
- mitigating regional conflicts; and
- promoting economic interests and improving the investment climate for foreign firms, including Russian companies.

Stated in more general terms, Trilateral countries have an abiding interest in a stable outcome in this fast-moving and potentially volatile region. Getting the mix of policies right is no easy task, for that mix cannot simply reinforce an inadequate status quo or attempt to bully skeptical leaders and publics toward Trilateral notions of democracy and free markets. It has to look beyond energy, but it is probably impossible to create such a mix without success in energy development. As a first step this mix requires a greater understanding of the region and the basis for Trilateral engagement.

However, no one should expect Trilateral interests and policies to be identical. Trilateral countries inevitably have different emphases in their approaches to this area. The EU, for instance, is much more concerned about drugs and migration from this area than is the United States, while the United States is much more concerned about non-proliferation issues than are the Europeans. The Trilateral states, as we conclude in the final chapter, could well play a decisive role in this region as a force for economic opportunity, global integration, and stability. These states could play this role precisely because no Trilateral country sees this region as a zone of vital interests. The derivative importance of this region is a great advantage in defining mutually reinforcing but distinctive Trilateral policies for a regional engagement without confrontation.

This introduction has laid out basic trends in the new Central Asia, as well as the challenges and interests Trilateral countries have to address and pursue. It is followed by chapters on U.S. (chapter II), Japanese (chapter III), and European (chapter IV) policies toward and involvement in the region. These chapters will attempt to weigh the various Trilateral policies and involvements against the challenges and interests described in this first chapter. The fifth and final chapter will provide a set of recommendations for Trilateral governments as they approach the new Central Asia.

II. The United States and the Caspian Basin

Sherman W. Garnett

The United States has articulated an ambitious, multi-faceted policy toward the states of the former Soviet South. U.S. policy focuses on what it calls the "Caspian Basin," a term encompassing portions of both Central Asia and the Caucasus. While seeking the development of the region's energy resources, including diversified export routes, this policy aims at much more than resource development. In recent years, senior officials in the Clinton Administration have defined their aims as nothing less than a transformation of the region itself and the international system around it. Explicitly rejecting the region's 19th century experience of the "Great Game," which pitted Britain against Russia in a contest for supremacy, U.S. Deputy Secretary of State Strobe Talbott stated in 1997, "Our goal is to avoid and actively to discourage that atavistic outcome....What we want to help bring about is just the opposite: We want to see all responsible players in the Caucasus and Central Asia be winners."[1]

Yet this ambitious policy faces formidable obstacles. Many states of the region face serious challenges to their stability, prosperity, and, perhaps, even their existence. Several have important oil and gas reserves, but these same regimes are marked by authoritarian and corrupt leaders, declining social services, poverty, backward transportation and communications links, and internal conflicts. They are located in a remote and challenging neighborhood, surrounded by larger powers, such as Turkey, Iran, Russia, and China, with historic traditions of engagement in and domination of the territories and peoples of these new states.

The states of the Caspian Basin, whether as participants in the global economy or as sources of instability, will doubtless influence regions and states far beyond the basin itself. U.S. policy embraces the goal of region-wide independence, global integration, and political and economic reforms. However, Russia, Iran, and other neighboring powers see U.S. support for regional transformation as a cover for an ambitious and hegemonic policy designed to exclude traditional actors and benefit Washington.

Moreover, the energy resources necessary to spur internal and regional transformation and global integration are themselves a question. Estimates have varied widely, from early enthusiasm for a possible "new Persian Gulf" to more sober recent assessments of oil reserves resembling those of the North Sea. The pipeline politics that would provide reliable transport of these resources to market are convoluted and delicate. And almost certainly the development of the region's natural wealth could just as easily exacerbate its political and social ills as mitigate them.

Obstacles to U.S. policy also come from within. No broad consensus exists on whether the region is truly critical to U.S. national interests. One analyst has divided those who do see a stake in the region—and they are by far a tiny minority of the American foreign policy community—into "oilers" and "geopoliticians."[2] The former see the region largely in terms of the resources it can produce. The latter, including the Clinton Administration, see oil as an instrument for larger political ends. Yet these larger ends are still underfunded and have yet to be embraced as a package by the states of the region themselves.

Add to these problems the distraction of U.S. presidential elections, widespread popular disinterest in foreign policy, and a pronounced shift in focus by the U.S. foreign policy community away from the former USSR. The end result is a series of questions: Beyond energy development, is the policy as ambitious as it seems? Does it fit both the region and U.S. interests there? Finally, is it sustainable, particularly as a new administration comes to power? Answers to these questions emerge only after a review of American policy toward the region.

A. THE BUILDING BLOCKS OF U.S. POLICY

The U.S. policy of broader engagement in the region has its roots in the Bush Administration. President Bush and his foreign policy team took the basic decisions to recognize the new states and establish formal diplomatic ties. The early focus of both Bush and Clinton Administrations on the establishment of a single nuclear successor to the Soviet Union brought Kazakhstan into early and sustained focus. Oil and gas also brought early attention to Kazakhstan and Azerbaijan. But the growth of a broad-based regional strategy—one defining the region for U.S. policy as the Caspian Basin—grows out of a 1997 policy review that brought the states of the Caspian region into clearer focus.

In subsequent interviews and testimony before Congress, senior Clinton Administration officials have described this ambitious U.S. policy for the region. This policy expands official interaction and assistance to current regimes, while promoting long-term democratic reforms, market liberalization, and human rights. U.S. regional efforts also focus on conflict resolution, security cooperation within the region and beyond it, and integration of this region into the global economy. The more detailed discussion below of these "building blocks" of U.S. policy uses the terms and categories outlined by the Clinton Administration.

Development of the region's oil, gas, and other natural resources is seen as a basic material support for these ends, as well as part of an overall U.S. energy policy of seeking diverse and secure sources of energy. U.S. policy assumes that Trilateral and regional interests coincide on these issues, even if there remain serious disagreements over pipeline routes and the division of the profits. U.S. officials stress that energy is not the be-all, end-all of American policy.

Assessments of the work done to implement this policy depend in part on whether one is examining the steady growth in U.S. assistance and involvement in the region from the low base-line of 1991 or the region's current needs and condition. As the following review makes plain, the picture is one of increased efforts but of even larger challenges and obstacles in the region.

1. Overall U.S. Assistance

The assistance the United States directly provides to the countries of the Caspian Basin is modest, even with recent and planned future increases. The major source of direct bilateral aid is the Freedom Support Act. The recent pattern of aid is presented in the Table II-1 below.

This chart is not exhaustive, because the United States also assists several of these countries through Nunn–Lugar funds for denuclearization, defense and security programs, and other sources. Nevertheless, it is indicative of the level of effort. Senior Administration officials characterized total aid efforts as "more than $2.2 billion" from 1992 until mid-1997 for the eight states of the Caucasus and Central Asia. Deputy Secretary Talbott spoke of $1.3 billion for Central Asia alone from 1992 to mid-1998.[3] At first glance, these levels appear to be far below what the stated policy would suggest or what the individual countries may need, but they are probably more than could be expected given the political mood of the U.S. Congress. Yet U.S. levels are in keeping with other international

TABLE II-1
U.S. Freedom Support Act Assistance
(US$ millions)

	FY1997 (actual)	FY1998 (actual)	FY1999 (estimate)	FY2000 (request)
Kazakhstan	35.5	40.5	44.2	53.5
Kyrgyzstan	20.8	24.5	28.5	34.5
Tajikistan	5.0	12.2	11.9	12.0
Turkmenistan	5.0	5.5	13.4	12.0
Uzbekistan	21.5	20.7	27.6	37.5
Azerbaijan	16.4	34.3	23.8	33.5
Central Asia Regional	0.6	7.9	11.3	11.5

Source: USAID Congressional presentations, www.info.usaid.gov/pubs/cp2000 and cp99.

programs. For example, Kazakhstan's IMF/World Bank recovery program is the largest in the region and is "roughly one-tenth" the smallest East Asian bailout. [4]

Local political and market conditions have suppressed the flow of foreign direct investment (FDI). Kazakhstan, to take perhaps the best case, received about $1.1 billion in net FDI inflows in 1996, with the United States the largest source of investment. In 1997, that figure rose modestly to $1.3 billion, with South Korea leading the way. More than 80 percent of FDI in 1993–97 was in hydrocarbons (50 percent by itself), metals, energy, and geological exploration.[5]

2. Increased Interaction and Engagement

Already under President Bush, once the fate of the USSR was clear, the United States decided to open embassies in every new capital. Secretary of Defense Cheney, often in the teeth of interagency opposition, made a similar commitment to staff each post with a defense attaché. Though rare visitors to Washington in the first years after independence, the presidents and senior officials from the Caspian Basin states now regularly visit Washington and other Trilateral capitals. President Nazarbayev visited Washington twice in the early years, May 1992 and February 1994, as part of the denuclearization process. Georgian President Shevardnadze came on a state visit in February 1994. President Clinton did not see President Niyazov of Turkmenistan during a private visit in this same period.

In 1997–98—the year after the U.S. policy review—the presidents of Azerbaijan, Georgia, Kazakhstan, Kyrgyzstan, and Turkmenistan visited Washington. The First Lady, Hillary Rodham Clinton, visited three Central Asian countries in October 1997. Cabinet Secretaries and senior U.S. officials with responsibilities for energy or regional issues regularly visit the regional capitals. Secretary Albright was in the region in April 2000, visiting Kazakhstan and Kyrgyzstan. Patterns of visits vary widely, with strategically and economically important states like Georgia, Azerbaijan, Kazakhstan, and Uzbekistan receiving a greater share of attention. Nonetheless, senior officials from these states are no longer strangers in Washington, and though summits are rare, working-level visits have become common.

3. Democratization and Human Rights

U.S. policy in this region aims, as it does globally, at democratic reforms and the respect of human rights. However, the former Soviet South is a region of few bright spots. Power is usually concentrated in the hands of a single leader. Parliaments are weak and easily manipulated. Elections are regular but rarely free and fair. In Azerbaijan, Kazakhstan, Turkmenistan, and Uzbekistan, the president has extended his power unilaterally or through Soviet-style elections in which turnout was high and the overwhelming support of the president a foregone conclusion. Tajikistan's politics have been dominated by the civil war and the fragile cease-fire and coalition agreement that has held since December 1996. Though the country no longer is rent by open conflict, it still experiences violence and chaos. Given the weakness of the central government, much of the country is only nominally under its control. Kyrgyzstan remains the sole bright spot, establishing the most open regime in the region.

In a 1997 speech, Deputy Secretary Talbott praised unconditionally only Georgia in his assessment of the state of democratization and human rights in the region. Since that time, dubious presidential elections in Armenia, Azerbaijan, and Kazakhstan and political violence in Armenia, Georgia, Tajikistan, and Uzbekistan have made conditions even worse.

No one expects the current regimes in the region to liberalize overnight. Small amounts of seed money are directed by USAID toward building stronger civil organizations and democratic institutions. ($6.2 million of the $53.5 million FY2000 Freedom

Support Act request for Kazakhstan is intended for democratization programs.[6]) U.S. NGOs are also at work at the grassroots level. Yet the trend line in the region, exacerbated by declining standards of living and social support, is largely negative.

Indeed, some supporters of U.S. engagement in the region argue that, given the internal and external challenges to the survival of these states, "preserving their independence has to take precedence over the immediate implementation of respect for human rights in their totality."[7] This debate over the relative importance of human rights and the standards that ought to be applied to states that fall short is nothing new to U.S. foreign policy and will doubtless continue to be a feature of any serious discussion of policy toward the region.

4. Market Reform

Large portions of Freedom Support Act assistance are aimed at supporting privatization and other market reforms. Nearly half of the FY99 request for Kazakhstan ($21.2 of $46 million) was in support of economic restructuring initiatives, the bulk going to privatization, legal and administrative reforms, and other technical assistance and training aimed at changing the business climate. The fact remains, however, that only Kyrgyzstan has obtained membership in the World Trade Organization. In Uzbekistan, for example, cumulative inflows of FDI probably did not exceed $250 million in the period from independence to 1995; and in 1996 and 1997, FDI was below $200 million per year. This low level of FDI is due in part to restrictive foreign exchange and trade policies and the deterioration of the business environment.[8] Corruption remains an enormous obstacle to business confidence. Over-regulation, confiscatory taxation, and competing central, regional, and local governmental rules and regulations make normal business practices impossible in many countries.

5. Conflict Resolution

The region is threatened by a number of armed conflicts. The instability in Afghanistan is felt throughout the Caspian Basin. Civil strife in Tajikistan and Georgia and the conflict which divides Azerbaijan and Armenia over Nagorno-Karabakh have all been frozen by cease-fire agreements, supplemented in some cases by multilateral peacekeeping and international observer missions. In each of these cases, there is no final resolution of the basic issues, and it seems doubtful that the basic elements of such a resolution can be found without outside support. These conflicts, plus the ongoing war in Chechnya and wider instability in the Russian North Caucasus, influence present or future pipeline routes. They cause untold human suffering and drain already scarce resources away from economic and social programs. U.S. policy aims at resolution of the region's conflicts as a basis for internal development and to prevent these conflicts from becoming a bone of contention between states within and outside the region.

The United States has taken a modest role in the UN mission to Georgia. In 1998, it provided four observers to the mission.[9] The United States has taken a more prominent role in the Nagorno-Karabakh conflict. Within the so-called Minsk process, U.S. diplomats work with their counterparts from France and Russia to negotiate with the parties of the conflict a long-term solution. Despite success in defining basic principles and narrowing differences, the two main interlocutors—Azerbaijan and Armenia—are deadlocked over key issues of end status for the province and basic procedure. One of the reasons for former Armenian President Ter-Petrosian's defeat in March 1998 presidential elections was his expressed willingness to pursue a Minsk Group compromise plan for Nagorno-Karabakh.

The United States has, however, carefully limited its role in supporting peacekeeping and other post-settlement arrangements. In part such caution is warranted, as U.S. troops would create concern for Russia and potentially introduce suspicion and friction among key parties to what will surely be an already complicated settlement. However, the inability of any indigenous or regional powers or institutions to carry the burden of such a settlement is obvious. The weak states of the region, warring factions, or a single neighboring power can not be expected to implement a comprehensive settlement.

6. Security Cooperation

The largest ongoing programs of military contacts and security cooperation between the United States and the states of the Caspian Basin are with Georgia, Uzbekistan, Kazakhstan, and, within the confines of U.S. legal limitations, Azerbaijan. These states, along with Ukraine, are seen by senior defense officials as keystone states in a policy of expanding security cooperation throughout the region of the former USSR. Expectations among these senior U.S. officials are modest, however, about security cooperation advancing beyond the current intensive effort in contacts, technical aid, and training.

The Central Asian states have recently been shifted from the U.S. European Command's Area of Operation to the Central Command, which has responsibility for the Persian Gulf and other areas of the

Middle East. Three Central Asian states—Kazakhstan, Kyrgyzstan, and Uzbekistan—were encouraged to form a joint peacekeeping battalion. The first exercises involving this battalion were held in the fall of 1997 at sites in Kazakhstan and Uzbekistan. A unit of the U.S. 82nd Airborne took part in the exercise, along with troops from Turkey, Georgia, Russia, and Latvia. The most recent exercise took place in Kazakhstan in September 2000, again with soldiers from the U.S. 82nd Airborne along with troops from Turkey, Georgia, Russia, Azerbaijan, Mongolia, and the United Kingdom.

However, the three Central Asian states have been slow to create a genuinely integrated unit, and they continue to squabble over headquarters and command arrangements. As a result, during visits to the region in late 1998 and 1999, senior U.S. defense and military officials encouraged the three countries to form separate battalions, which could in turn operate with each other or other peacekeeping forces. The incident reflects the difficulties within the region that stand in the way of the kind of security cooperation the United States and its NATO allies have encouraged elsewhere. The regional ambitions and rivalries of the three participating states will likely continue to prevent them from forming a truly cooperative security arrangement and thus will retard U.S. cooperative efforts, for Washington does not want to appear to be favoring one state over the other. In particular, it does not want to be seen as favoring one party over another in the intense Kazakh–Uzbek rivalry for security primacy in the region.

U.S. Congressional restrictions—Section 907—have placed severe limits on security and other forms of cooperation beyond humanitarian aid with Azerbaijan. Congressionally mandated sanctions have been imposed in response to Azerbaijan's blockade of Armenia as a result of the Nagorno-Karabakh war. The Clinton Administration has consistently sought to repeal or soften these restrictions but has failed to persuade Congress. Despite these restrictions, U.S.–Azerbaijani security cooperation remains a priority, even if now it must be limited to expanded contacts and the few forms of assistance permitted by the law.

But the most important limitation on cooperation may simply be the remoteness of these regions from the first order concerns of the U.S. military. The U.S. Central Command has responsibility for the Persian Gulf, making it a sure bet that security cooperation with states like Kazakhstan cannot occupy too high a place in the in-box of the most senior military commanders.

7. Global Integration

U.S. policy also aims at encouraging the integration of the states of the Caspian Basin into the global economy and world community. Zbigniew Brzezinski described the U.S. role as essentially twofold: "to preserve the independence of the new states and to maximize the opportunities for their inclusion in the world economic system and in some rudimentary structure of international security."[10] Thus U.S. officials urge regional leaders to see their domestic reforms in the light of eventual membership in institutions like the WTO. The stability, independence, and integration of these states into the larger world is seen as a boost for Russia's own stability and self-definition.[11] It prevents the region from becoming a power vacuum that would draw Russia, China, Iran, and others into a dangerous competition for influence.

8. Energy and Other Economic Interests

Despite efforts to place energy issues within a larger strategic context, oil and gas remain by far the clearest stake and the most powerful driver of U.S. policy. Indeed, the more ambitious regional strategy presupposes the success of this enterprise as a foundation for political and economic transformation of the region. Under Secretary of State Eizenstat encapsulated this notion in his 1997 testimony to Congress:

> While estimates of the size of regional oil and gas reserves vary widely, the Caspian Sea is potentially one of the world's most important new energy-producing regions. Although the Caspian may never rival the Persian Gulf, Caspian production can have important implications for world energy supplies on the margins. We believe rapid development of these energy resources and trade linkages is critical to the independence, prosperity, democracy, and stability of all the countries of Central Asia and the Caucasus.[12]

Energy is the driving force for U.S. companies involved in the region. The bulk of U.S. FDI has been aimed at energy producers—Kazakhstan and Azerbaijan in particular—and at energy and energy-related projects within those countries. Large multinational energy firms are competing and cooperating to bring oil and natural gas to market. Among U.S.-based firms, Chevron and ExxonMobil and others have been active in the major fields of Kazakhstan and Azerbaijan. A wide range of U.S. firms have taken part in the search for energy or in the provision of essential support services. These efforts will only increase with new finds, for instance in the wake of promising reports from test drilling in the Kashagan formation in Kazakhstan. Future development of oil and gas fields and the construction of new pipelines will continue to attract U.S. firms.

Large American consumer-oriented companies, such as Coca-Cola and Procter & Gamble, are active in the region. So are the manufacturers of agricultural and heavy equipment, like John Deere. Indeed, in the long run, agricultural investment promises substantial pay-off, both for outside investors and the local economies in places like Uzbekistan and Kazakhstan. But near- and medium-term U.S. economic interests are largely defined by oil and gas and the support their extraction and transportation require.

The cities of Almaty, Baku, and Tashkent are being transformed by the influx of investment and the anticipation of more wealth to come. Energy development has brought with it a host of related support businesses, from communications to construction. New hotels, restaurants, and other services have come into being to support the foreign business community. New flights have been added to Central Asia by major air carriers, though the transportation network to support them still lags behind. There is little doubt that, if energy development is a success, it has the potential to be a leading edge of job and wealth creation in the region, eventually supporting a more broad-based economic engagement that will no longer be so dependent on oil and gas.

Yet most analysts predict that the reality of future oil and gas wealth will be more limited than some had earlier imagined. While Caspian energy resources are significant, recent estimates have reigned in earlier speculation that the region might become a second Persian Gulf. By 2010, Caspian oil "will account for less than 5 percent of global oil consumption."[13] The costs of exploration, development, and transportation are likely to be relatively high.

Of greatest concern, however, is that the current political and economic infrastructure is simply not likely to turn oil and gas money into broad and sustainable economic development. There is already widespread speculation that existing corruption, nepotism, and clan-politics will hoard newfound oil wealth or transfer it out of the country rather than turn it to economically and socially productive investments and services. Unless politics change radically in many of these countries, energy wealth will only add to social ills and political instability. These effects go well beyond the economic distortions seen in some Trilateral countries in earlier decades when energy wealth inflated consumer prices and undermined the steady development of indigenous agricultural, manufacturing, and service sectors. Senior energy company executives are also concerned about political factors both in the region and in Washington. They are concerned about the absence of clear successors for the region's current aging leaders, and they also bristle at U.S. government efforts to place geopolitical considerations ahead of commercial viability in the determination of pipeline routes. These energy executives are convinced that multiple pipelines will eventually be developed, if prudent estimates of reserves are confirmed. They would prefer, however, that the pattern of multiple pipelines emerge as a result of market forces.

These less-than-rosy trend lines for the region make U.S. energy companies even more hard-headed in their pursuit of viable and profitable arrangements for development and transport of energy. It makes them wary of ambitious geopolitical notions attached to pipelines and energy wealth that will add to an already expensive price tag. For instance, it makes them cautious of endorsing the Baku–Ceyhan pipeline project. Indeed, most have seen their interest best served in insisting that commercial viability be the most important determinant of pipeline routes. These companies are quite used to managing high risks and political instability. However, they do not want to take on the additional missions and responsibilities implied in the overarching U.S. regional policy.

There is thus a tension between the leading U.S. economic actors in the region and U.S. government policy. That tension has been softened or obscured at times, but remains, especially over pipelines. Most private actors emphasize the least costly solutions for pipelines regardless of geopolitics, including pipelines through Russia. They point to the commercial logic of eventual Iranian routes. The Clinton Administration continues to argue for the pipeline from Baku to Ceyhan in Turkey as "one of the multiple routes."[14] Normalization of relations with Iran is potentially the most important long-term factor in the energy transportation equation. However, even the most optimistic view of U.S.–Iranian normalization sees it as a slow process, taking years. Near-term decisions on alternative pipelines are unlikely to be transformed by a dramatic U.S.–Iranian breakthrough.

B. CHALLENGES TO U.S. POLICY

By comparison with other Trilateral efforts in the region, U.S. policy is ambitious. No other Trilateral state has articulated such a wide-ranging and interlocking set of interests and goals for the region. Yet three basic questions remain. Does this policy correctly understand the region and U.S. interests there? Does it have the right mix of programs and resources to support its aims? And, finally, is it sustainable for the United States?

With regard to the first question, U.S. policy has lumped the countries of the former Soviet South into a single region, centered on the Caspian Sea. The focus on the Caspian underscores the centrality of energy development to Washington's working definition of the region. Yet there are serious questions whether these countries are in fact a single region at all. They are not all energy-rich or even Islamic. They have very different histories and traditions, as well as different trajectories. China is crucial to the future of Kazakhstan and Kyrgyzstan but hardly worth a thought in the Caucasus, where Iran and Turkey are center-stage. Though they are all former Soviet republics, this common past is quickly becoming individualized and fragmented. The future is likely to see three or four different geopolitical orientations emerge, as Russian, Chinese, Turkish, Iranian, and Trilateral influences work upon vastly different states and economic zones.

The most serious challenges to such ambitious policy aims come from the weaknesses of these states. In the words of one leading analyst, these countries face "...a set of daunting developmental challenges unlike those in most other postcolonial countries."[15] These include declining standards of living, health, and education; the growing number of citizens living below the poverty line; ethnic and religious tensions; and the complication of geographic remoteness from the developed world. The very political trends that have guaranteed near-term stability—strong and authoritarian-minded presidents and highly personalized regimes—could easily become a longer-term source of instability. The passing of these leaders from the scene—several are of advanced age and others have been the targets of assassins—would expose the weak state institutions and sources of instability that lie beneath one-man rule. The region could also see the breakdown of the cease-fires that have frozen the existing conflicts in the area.

The region's very complexity and remoteness raise important questions about how vital U.S. interests there are. The desirability of energy development is clear, but whether the policy articulated by the Clinton Administration genuinely rests on a defensible set of long-term U.S. interests is less clear. It is doubted whether even well-informed members of the U.S. foreign policy community know much about these states or U.S. policy toward them. In the years ahead, more will be required than occasional visits, parachute jumps, and position papers to have the impact desired. Indeed, a serious crisis in the region will almost certainly separate wheat from chaff in U.S. policy, as Washington decides whether to be an engaged participant or a sideline observer. Most analysts bet that, in such a crisis, the United States will likely limit its exposure. Energy companies in the United States and elsewhere are capable of pursuing their interests in the area without being part of a larger effort at political and economic transformation. Senior officials at these companies cultivate the region's current leaders, even as they anticipate change and even instability. Oil and gas will have a dynamic of their own.

U.S. policy depends on understanding the region and long-term commitment to it, at a time when the world's only true superpower has an enormous range of other commitments and interests that are more clearly defined and much better understood by the American public.

The strongest case for sustained U.S. involvement is probably not a generic appeal to democratization and market reform—a long and unsure process at best—but an understanding of cultural, commercial, and political trends that will over time link one or more of the states in Central Asia and the Caucasus to issues of vital importance. These include the stability of Turkey and the Persian Gulf, the direction of Russia's internal development and external posture, and the role, positive or negative, that China will play. The transformation of this inner-Asian region into "the Eurasian Balkans" would have effects on the outer rim of Asia that are still not understood or imagined by those who have no idea where Tashkent or Bishkek are. As ambitious as U.S. policy statements are, they fail in articulating the trends that are likely to give the region its security importance for the United States in the years ahead.

That policy also fails to place its hopes for pluralistic political developments within a recognizable regional context. Even as economic interests dictate flirtation with regimes that are unsteady and unlikely to last, U.S. political interests (and incidentally the interests of Russia and China) require a broad-based accommodation with and encouragement of moderate Islam. The notion current in many quarters of both governmental and public opinion that Islamicization inevitably brings radicalization and anti-Americanism displays a powerful ignorance of these countries and the varieties of Islamic worship and culture that lie at the region's historical roots. The region still awaits a creative effort to engage Islam with the best of Western democratic and pluralistic political traditions. A sustained effort at this encounter will have broader, positive value for U.S. interests throughout the Islamic world.

U.S. policy also fails to take account of the "geopolitical pluralism" already at work in redefining the region. The normal development of the region needs a healthy and engaged Turkey, which is in fact a centerpiece of U.S. policy, but it also requires normalized roles for Russia, Iran, and China. Cooperation with Russia is complicated. Russian leaders and foreign policy analysts tend to see U.S. policy as a direct challenge to their interests. Successful encouragement of Russian energy companies, which have shown themselves willing to play by the accepted rules of the game in the energy development and transportation of the region, is a key. But so is weaning Russia away from seeing its southern neighbors in old-fashioned security terms. Russia and the United States share a common interest in seeing this important region in Russia's backyard prosperous and stable. The obstacle to this is not U.S.–Russian competition for influence, but weak states, corruption, economic backwardness, and civil strife. Iran has played a surprisingly positive role in this region, placing its own concerns about Afghanistan and regional stability ahead of ideological interests. China too has become more deeply engaged, especially as an economic actor and a cooperative partner on security with Russia and Central Asian border states. There are no signs that Sino–U.S. ties have focused on Central Asia at all.

Little needs to be said in answer to the second question beyond the obvious discrepancy between ambitious rhetoric and rather meager foreign assistance. A wide range of critics of U.S. foreign policy have underscored the low levels of foreign aid to needy regions of the world. This region is no exception. The efforts, though expanding, are still low. No genuine engagement with the region, barring an indigenous economic turnaround and flood of private investment, is possible on these levels of assistance. More sweeping criticism may also be made of the programs themselves, particularly those that promote our political and economic ideals in seeming ignorance of local conditions and past practices. In fact, unless some greater effectiveness is achieved here, both in the amount of aid and in the kinds of programs offered, U.S. policy will increasingly seem to the leaders and people of the region as nothing more than grandiloquent policy pronouncements.

The third question looms large during the current election season. However, it is doubtful whether a new Administration, even a new Republican Administration, will greatly alter its stance toward the key states of the region (Kazakhstan, Uzbekistan, Georgia, Azerbaijan). Some on the Republican side might find them more attractive as part and parcel of a "hedge against Russia." However, the mainstream of either party in the White House is less likely to err on the side of over-commitment in the name of the "quarantine" of Russia, than on the side of neglect and lack of concern. New energy finds, the maturing of U.S. investment in the region, and a longer-term breakthrough with Iran could alter Washington's level of engagement; but it is unlikely to reach the level of U.S.–Ukrainian ties, the most ambitious U.S. engagement in the post-Soviet space outside of Russia.

U.S. policy lacks a strong and sustainable domestic consensus, though the key irritant is not political or party differences. "Oilers" are primarily interested in energy development, not geopolitics. Strong Armenian-American efforts have kept Section 907 restrictions on aid to Azerbaijan in place. There is little support for conflict resolution efforts that would involve expensive and potentially dangerous deployments of U.S. forces into conflict zones in this remote region. Congressional suspicion of foreign assistance will almost certainly limit U.S. aid.

In sum, the Clinton Administration has articulated, for itself and for its successor, an ambitious policy for a remote region. It and its successor will have other challenges and distractions widely seen as involving more important national interests than those at stake in the Caspian Basin. In an era when U.S. credibility will be questioned and challenged throughout the globe, this policy could easily become hollow. Given these problems, some impetus toward a common Trilateral strategic approach, a more conscientious effort at pooling scarce resources and the creation of a sensible and reinforcing division of labor ought to be a higher priority.

C. THE WAY AHEAD

The best way to sustain a sensible engagement in the region is to understand the weaknesses of the current policy, particularly its over-ambitious and generic declarations and its under-appreciation of the challenges ahead.

There are reasons for a sustained engagement toward the region. Energy resources are among them. Oil and gas represent both a common and competitive interest for all the Trilateral countries and their respective companies. These companies have pursued both competition and cooperation with gusto and need little help from their governments in understanding the opportunities and assessing the risks of energy development and transportation in the region.

As energy development proceeds, whether at a fast or more measured pace, the key issue will be whether the Caspian Basin, as it comes into increasing interaction with the outside world will do so as an exporter of energy or of instability, as states seeking to integrate into the modern global economy or as basket cases hopelessly apart from it. The recent history of neighboring Afghanistan provides an obvious example of a development path inimical to Trilateral interests. The key challenge for the states of the region themselves, for their neighbors and for the Trilateral countries will be to maintain stability, encourage economic growth and integration, and promote pluralism and democratization.

A stable region will have a huge impact on Russia's own perceptions of the changes going on inside and around it. If Trilateral countries can help to stabilize a region of significance to Russia—and find ways to work cooperatively with Russia toward that goal—this process would go a long way toward soothing Russian suspicions that the United States and other Trilateral states are seeking to displace Russia from the region and to take economic advantage at Russia's expense.

A stable region will also have a positive impact on Turkey, Iran, China, and South Asia. It would remove a source of potential friction and competition. If a "Great Game" were to re-emerge in the region, it would most likely not involve any of the Trilateral states but these great neighboring states. A competition of Russia, China, Iran, and Turkey or any two of this set would have enormous implications for Eurasian stability, energy security, trade, and proliferation of advanced weapons and possibly even weapons of mass destruction. The cause of heading off this competition is not served by the isolation of Iran, even though its support of terrorism and its nuclear ambitions do not justify full normalization.

Yet even the most farsighted U.S. policy toward the region cannot be sustained without greater cooperation with interested parties, especially Trilateral partners and institutions. Coordination of efforts and, where possible, pooling of resources would have an important multiplier effect on assistance, exchanges, and technical advice that will likely remain limited in comparison with regions and countries of higher priority for Trilateral countries.

The view of the potential strategic significance of the region beyond its oil resources is one that ought to be shared by all Trilateral

CANADIAN POLICY TOWARD THE NEW CENTRAL ASIA

Canada has not taken as active a role in the Central Asian region as it has in the Baltic States and Ukraine. The countries of Central Asia and the Caucasus are "not a part of the world in which Canada has been extensively engaged," admits James R. Wright, Director General for Central, South, and East Europe of the Ministry of Foreign Affairs and International Trade.[16]

Canada maintains but a single embassy in the region, in Kazakhstan. Growing from a small trade post, the embassy has expanded to a full-service diplomatic post with three Canada-based officers (including one from CIDA). Its personnel are also accredited to Kyrgyzstan and Tajikistan. As for the rest of the region, Canadian diplomats in Ankara cover Azerbaijan and Turkmenistan (and Georgia); its Moscow personnel also cover Uzbekistan (and Armenia). This arrangement admittedly gives Canada less day-to-day influence over much of the region than Trilateral countries with permanent diplomatic missions in additional capitals. This shortfall in Canadian diplomatic support also has commercial implications in a region where government-to-government relations are often key to getting and sustaining access to the unpredictable markets of the region.

In fact, commercial interests, especially in energy and mineral resources, have largely defined Ottawa's approach to the region. Canadian firms are involved in developing Kazakhstan's and Azerbaijan's energy sector, both directly in oil and gas field development[17] and indirectly in services (such as helicopter transport to and from offshore platforms). Canada's gold mining companies—such as Barrick, Placer Dome, Cameco and Teck—are especially active in Central Asia. Cameco Gold is the largest single Canadian investor in the former USSR and the largest investor in Kyrgyzstan.

Canadian expertise is at work on the Aral Sea remediation effort, an example of an expanding range of technical assistance Ottawa now provides to the region. The Canadian government has expressed its support for human rights, democratization, and economic reform efforts in the region. It has supported regional anti-drug and cooperative law enforcement programs. Senior Canadian diplomats recognize the need to expand Ottawa's presence in the region, though budget constraints and other foreign policy priorities seem likely to make such an expansion a long-term process at best.

parties. For the stakes in the region are higher than simply whether oil, gas, and other natural resources come to market. The region will have a profound impact on Russian and Chinese stability, identity, and interests in the coming century. A positive-sum, commercially oriented outcome will help diffuse suspicions in Moscow and Beijing of U.S. and Western hegemony. It would help the region break free from its past of external domination and internal underdevelopment. The main determinant of such an outcome will be the policies of the states of the region themselves, but the United States and its Trilateral partners have a key role to play as well.

III. JAPAN AND THE NEW CENTRAL ASIA

Koji Watanabe

A. INTRODUCTION

Contrary to a widely held perception in both the United States and Europe, Japan's policy of engagement with Central Asia is not motivated primarily by economic or commercial interests. Rather, it is based upon political considerations characterized by a benign sense of friendship to these newly independent nations of the former Soviet Union. The Asian identity of the peoples in the region as well as their leaders' ardent plea for assistance with economic reform have moved Japanese decision-makers to provide substantial amounts of Official Development Assistance (ODA) to the region and especially to two countries, namely Kyrgyzstan and Uzbekistan, both of which lack major oil and gas resources.

Indeed, there is a near consensus in Japanese business circles that the Central Asian countries have little attraction as markets for Japanese goods, something that is unlikely to change in the foreseeable future. Furthermore, while there is no doubt that the Caspian Basin is richly endowed in oil and gas, which if developed properly could bring prosperity to the region and help stabilize it politically, Japanese investment remains quite modest certainly compared to U.S., European, and Chinese involvement. The region's oil and gas reserves are not likely to play a significant if any role in meeting Japan's energy needs in the future principally because of the enormous transportation challenges involved. Overall then, Japan's business interest and presence in the region could hardly be sustained without the substantial economic assistance provided by the Japanese government to the region.

What then are motivating forces behind such a benign policy of engagement? First and foremost, there is a genuine wish on the part of the Japanese government to help promote the development of a stable and independent group of nations in Central Asia surrounded as they are by the major powers of Eurasia. For Japan, as a major industrial democracy seeking to play a constructive role in the post-Cold War era, there was virtually no choice but to respond positively to the earnest requests for assistance by the leaders of this distant but nonetheless Asian region. In this respect, a parallel can be drawn with Japan's close cooperative relationship with Mongolia. Since the early 1990s Japan has been the largest donor of foreign aid to Mongolia, whose fiscal budget has been largely sustained by Japanese economic assistance. Yet Mongolia's attractiveness as a commercial market for Japan is of very modest magnitude.

Another factor influencing Japan's engagement in Central Asia has been the wish to maintain and develop stable and hopefully friendly relations with Russia, China, Turkey, and Iran. Japan believes that these major players surrounding the region as well as the G-7 countries all share a basic interest in a stable Central Asia, even though they may wish to increase their respective influence. The benign motives driving Japan's policy toward Central Asia will hopefully contribute to it enjoying better relations with those countries.

B. OVERVIEW

Japan's involvement in Central Asia during the Soviet era had been negligible largely because of the politics of the Cold War and the region's geographical separation from Japan. However, after the former Soviet republics gained their independence following the dissolution of the Soviet Union at the end of 1991, Japan's involvement began to increase steadily as manifested by the level of official contacts and, moreover, economic assistance. As indicated above, these developed in response to the strong pleas for assistance in introducing market-oriented economic reforms by such leaders as President Akayev of Kyrgystan, who made his first official visit to Japan in 1993, followed by President Nazarbayev of Kazakhstan and President Karimov of Uzbekistan in 1994.

As a consequence, Japan became one of the major donors of ODA to Central Asia together with the United States and Germany. Also, with the encouragement of the Japanese government, Japanese business circles began developing joint economic committees with government and business leaders of four Central Asian countries—excluding Tajikistan—and Azerbaijan. These economic committees now meet annually, alternating between Japan and the respective Central Asian capitals.

Japan's growing involvement in Central Asia culminated with a major policy speech by then Japanese Prime Minister Ryutaro Hashimoto in June 1997. In what subsequently became called the "Eurasian" or "Silk Road" diplomacy, Hashimoto laid out the reasons for Japan's policy of engagement with the Central Asian Republics and the nations of the Caucasus region.

Japan's Central Asia policy is based upon three basic considerations which are believed to warrant substantial Japanese engagement in the region:

- Given that Central Asia is geopolitically important for the stability of all Eurasia, surrounded as it is by Russia, the Middle East, and China, a policy of constructive engagement to promote stability is not only important for international peace in general but can also be instrumental in shaping positive and constructive relations with Russia and China, Japan's two important neighbors, as well as Middle Eastern countries, notably Turkey and Iran.

- Caspian Sea energy resources of oil and natural gas are in all likelihood of a magnitude that will substantially affect the global energy landscape. Developing these resources could serve to diversify energy supply sources for Asian countries, including Japan. Diversification away from over-dependence on Middle East oil is a major long-term concern for East Asian countries.

- The absence of a negative historical involvement with the region and Japan's long-held status as the only modern advanced industrial country in Asia produced a benign and positive image of Japan among political elites in the region. The high expectations placed upon Japan have been reciprocated by nostalgic sentiments among the Japanese public, who consider the Central Asian peoples as historically close Asian friends who once played a crucial role in the Great Silk Road.

Japan's engagement with countries in Central Asia has nevertheless proven to be uneven. As the first visit by a head of state from a Central Asian republic to Japan was made by President Akayev, Japan's engagement in the region started in Kyrgyzstan. Reflecting President Akayev's strong desire to establish close cooperative relations with Japan as well as Japan's appreciation for his democratic and reformist orientation, Japan subsequently became the largest ODA donor to that country. The fact that Kyrgyz people are strikingly similar to Japanese in physical appearance has not hurt this relationship.

Relations with Kazakhstan and Uzbekistan followed. Both republics have received substantial assistance from Japan, but Uzbekistan has been more emphatic about the positive effect of the assistance; Kazakhstan tends to consider Japanese assistance helpful but not essential. Japan played an important role in initiating development assistance to Uzbekistan in 1994, thus paving the way for U.S. and World Bank assistance to the republic, whose "gradualist" approach toward economic reform had not previously appealed to the two donors.

Until recently, Japan's engagement with Tajikistan and Turkmenistan has been less pronounced than with the other three republics. Tajikistan had high expectations for Japanese assistance and has been most appreciative of Japan's humanitarian and technical assistance program in the form of Japan's accepting trainees from the war-torn country. Japan's concern for the restoration of peace in that country prompted its decision to send Dr. Yutaka Akino, a highly respected university professor, to the United Nations Mission of Observers in Tajikistan (UNMOT) as UN political officer in the spring of 1998. When he was killed by rebels in the countryside, the shock in Japan was overwhelming. If only to commemorate his devotion, the Japanese government has decided to expand drastically the technical assistance program by inviting hundreds of trainees in various fields from Tajikistan.

Japan's involvement with Turkmenistan has developed only recently, but the ties are expected to strengthen because of the potential for developing energy resources. Similarly, with the participation of a Japanese firm in the Azerbaijian International Operating Company (AIOC), Japanese interest in Azerbaijan has rapidly increased. President Aliyev visited Japan in February 1998. After the visit the first yen credit loan was granted for the construction of a gas-powered electricity-generating plant.

In August 1999, four Japanese mining experts sent by the Japan International Cooperation Agency (JICA) to Kyrgyzstan as part of a technical assistance program for gold and copper mining exploration were kidnapped and detained for two months as hostages by Islamic militant forces in the southern part of Kyrgyzstan south of the Ferghana Valley bordering on Tajikistan. The Islamic militants were identified as anti-government forces in Uzbekistan who had fled to Tajikistan from Uzbekistan. They were on their way back to Uzbekistan since their activities in Tajikistan had become increasingly difficult due to an agreement reached between the Tajik government and anti-government forces to disarm the latter by August 24. The incident, which became a major national concern in Japan, was resolved by major efforts by the Kyrgyz government, revealing the very nature of instability in the region around the Ferghana Valley and the potent danger posed by Islamic militants.

C. CURRENT POLITICAL OBJECTIVES AND CONCERNS

Besides providing economic assistance to the region, Japan's current policy of engagement has other facets. In particular it entails promoting political dialogue to enhance mutual trust and understanding, expanding economic cooperation and development of the region's natural resources so as to foster prosperity, and contributing to building peace through nuclear non-proliferation, democratization, and the fostering of stability.

It so happened that in July 1997, just prior to Hashimoto's speech, Mr. Keizo Obuchi, who subsequently became Prime Minister in August 1998, led a large friendship mission to Central Asian countries in his capacity as a senior parliamentarian. The mission, composed of parliamentarians, government officials, businessmen, and academics, visited four Central Asian countries, excluding Tajikistan. Mr. Obuchi established a good personal rapport with leaders of the region and, in summing up his visit to Central Asia, stressed the importance of continued political dialogue and economic cooperation with the countries of the region in their nation-building efforts.

The major political objective behind Japanese efforts has been to assist the maintenance of peace and independence of the emerging nation-states in this geostrategically important region. Providing technical and economic assistance to the countries of the region has been the primary instrument for doing this. As the world's largest ODA donor nation, Japan took the initiative in the Organization for Economic Cooperation and Development (OECD) to make the countries in Central Asia eligible for ODA in 1993 and the three Caucasus countries eligible in 1994.

In 1996 Japan also hosted in Tokyo a World Bank meeting of donor countries for Kazakhstan, Kyrgyzstan, and Tajikistan, to which the prime ministers of the three countries were invited and engaged in political dialogue with Japanese political and business leaders.

Reflecting its strong concern over nuclear pollution, in August 1999 the Japanese government convened with the joint sponsorship of the

United Nations Development Program (UNDP) the Tokyo International Conference on Semipalatinsk. With the participation of twenty-four countries, the conference succeeded in focusing international attention on the plight of people of the region suffering the aftereffects of nuclear testing. The Kazakh government particularly appreciated this. Also, the Japanese government and Japanese non-governmental organizations are conducting studies on the issue of environmental pollution in the Aral Sea, although efforts are not progressing smoothly owing to a lack of consensus among the countries concerned.

The situation in Tajikistan is a source of political concern for Japan, accentuated by the brutal murder of Professor Akino and the kidnapping of four Japanese by Uzbek militants fleeing from Tajikistan. The recently held election in Tajikistan in which anti-government forces participated would be a welcome sign if it could signify the beginning of the stabilization process. The election was significant in the sense that never in the past had an election been held in Central Asia that allowed the former Islamic militants to participate peacefully. In the event, under the joint observation of UNMOT and OSCE, the Islamic Renaissance Party led by Said Abdullo Nuri gained 7 percent of the votes. As a sign of keen interest in the peace and reconciliation process, the Japanese government has sent Keizo Takemi, a senior parliamentarian who served until recently as Parliamentary Vice Minister for Foreign Affairs, as an election-observer.

One of the remarkable developments in Tajikistan is the substantial success of UNMOT in disarming anti-Government forces, which made the election possible. In the view of many observers, the crucial task now is how to rehabilitate the disarmed militants and provide them viable job opportunities. The Japanese government is now prepared to cooperate with the UNDP and UNTOP (the successor of UNMOT, whose mandate expired on May 15) in their job-creation and rehabilitation programs, so that those former militants would not threaten the fragile stability again. The OSCE could also play a crucial role in human rights protection and the Japanese authorities are currently discussing with OSCE representatives as to how to help those who have suffered from the internal disturbances for such a long time.

Finally, on the premise that the situation in Afghanistan is linked in important ways to the situation in Tajikistan, the Japanese government has participated in various UN efforts to bring peace to that country by sending political officers to the respective UN missions.

D. CURRENT ECONOMIC INTERESTS AND INVOLVEMENT

Due to its distance from Japan, the transportation costs involved and the small size of the market, Central Asia has few economic or commercial attractions to Japanese business interests. The only exception is the energy resources of the Caspian Basin, but even here Japanese involvement has been slow and remains limited. Though Japanese companies have shown increasing interest in taking the initiative in the development of energy resources in Azerbaijan and Kazakhstan, they are not yet major players in the region. The distance makes it difficult to transport extracted oil and gas to Japan, and Japanese companies are relatively inexperienced in exploiting oil and gas resources.

Trade relations between Japan and the Central Asia region are consequently not substantial (see Table III-1) and Japanese direct investment is meager.

It is remarkable in this sense that Japan is among the major donors to Kyrgyzstan, Uzbekistan, and, to a lesser extent, Kazakhstan. Japanese government support and assistance have taken three forms: humanitarian and development assistance (ODA); Export-Import Bank credits; and encouragement to Japanese business circles to expand trade and economic relations.

Among three forms of ODA, two—the so-called technical assistance program and humanitarian assistance—have been extended to the Central Asia and Caucasus regions. Actually, both forms of assistance were extended as part of common efforts by G-7 summit countries to assist the Newly Independent States (NIS) of the former Soviet Union. Accepting trainees from and sending technical experts to these countries was announced in April 1993 as part of US$12 million in assistance to promote reform in the NIS.

In the light of the importance of assistance in the field of software for the countries in transition from socialist regimes to market economies, the Japanese Government announced in early 1993 acceptance of 300 trainees for three years from five Central Asian countries. By the end of 1995, 303 trainees had been accepted. Since then, 100 trainees have been invited annually from the region for acquiring knowledge and practice of market reform and administrative management. Japan's technical assistance program also sends experts in economic management as well as communications, banking, environment, and transportation infrastructure.

TABLE III-1

Japan's Trade with Central Asia and the Caucasus, 1998

(US$ thousands)

	Exports to Japan	Imports from Japan	Trade Balance
Uzbekistan	40,965	68,344	-27,379
Kazakhstan	122,279	54,077	68,201
Kyrgyzstan	551	1,105	-554
Turkmenistan	23	8,005	-7,982
Tajikistan	61	5,397	-5,336
Subtotal	**163,880**	**136,931**	**26,949**
Azerbaijan	218	19,243	-19,025
Georgia	675	3,304	-2,629
Armenia	5,963	1,917	4,046
Subtotal	**6,857**	**24,465**	**-17,608**
Total	**170,738**	**161,397**	**9,341**

Note: US$1=¥128.28

Official development loans with concessionary terms are being extended to all countries in the region, except Tajikistan and Armenia, in the fields of transportation, communication, and energy development. Grant assistance has been given to the medical and health-care sectors, along with non-project fiscal support assistance and grassroots assistance.

The major objective of economic assistance is to actively support the efforts of those countries to introduce market-oriented economies. Particular emphasis is placed on human resources development in the case of technical assistance and on the alleviation of difficulties involved in the process of economic reform in the case of financial assistance. More specifically, development assistance prioritizes four sectors: market reform; infrastructure-building in transportation and communication; medical welfare and education; and environment protection, including, notably, the Aral Sea.

It is to be noted that the Japanese government's development loans for Central Asian countries concentrate on infrastructure-building in transportation and communication, while those for countries in the Caucasus region are for energy sector projects that contribute to the improvement of their respective balance-of-payment situations.

As shown by Table III-2, the total amount of ODA disbursed from 1993 through 1997 was US$356 million. The total amount pledged was ¥135.8 billion.

Aside from ODA, Japanese Export-Import Bank credits amounting to ¥220 billion are playing a very important role in the modernization of plants and equipment in the Central Asia/Caucasus countries. The credits take the form of either untied loans in conjunction with IMF or World Bank loans or import financing for plants and equipment. They include de-sulphurization equipment for Uzbek oil refineries in Bukhara and Ferghana, a raw cotton processing plant in Turkmenistan, and modernization equipment for an ether plant in Azerbaijan.

As noted earlier, Japanese business circles have established joint economic committees with each of four Central Asian countries and Azerbaijan through which government and business leaders meet annually. While the Central Asian delegations are usually represented by the prime minister or deputy prime minister, the Japanese delegation is led by the chief executive officer or the chairman of the

TABLE III-2
Japanese ODA Disbursements to
Central Asia and the Caucasus, 1993–97
(US$ millions)

	1993	1994	1995	1996	1997	Total
Grant Aid	—	0.49 (0.0%)	21.87 (0.7%)	33.09 (1.4%)	41.46 (2.1%)	96.91
Technical Cooperation	2.57 (0.1%)	8.97 (0.3%)	14.97 (0.4%)	18.8 (0.6%)	24.54 (0.8%)	69.85
Subtotal	**2.57** (0.1%)	**9.46** (0.2%)	**36.84** (0.6%)	**51.88** (0.9%)	**66.01** (1.3%)	**166.76**
Loan Aid	—	39.73 (0.9%)	30.45 (0.7%)	28.13 (0.1%)	90.87 (5.8%)	189.18
Total	**2.57** (0.0%)	**49.19** (0.5%)	**67.29** (0.6%)	**80.01** (0.1%)	**156.88** (2.4%)	**355.94**

Note: The percentages in parentheses represent shares of overall grant aid, overall technical cooperation, and overall ODA loans for that year.

board of directors of a leading trading firm, i.e. Mitsubishi for Kazakhstan, Mitsui for Uzbekistan, Sumitomo for Kyrgyzstan, Itochu for Turkmenistan, and Nichimen for Azerbaijan. These committees serve the useful purpose of providing a regular opportunity for leaders of the region to visit Japan and engage in dialogue with Japanese leaders.

Japanese firms are interested in participating in oil and gas development projects in the Caspian Basin. So far their records have not been dramatic, however. Itochu, a company strongly interested in Caspian oil, holds about 4 percent of the largest project to date in Azerbaijan, the AIOC (Azerbaijani International Operating Company) consortium developing the offshore Azeri–Chirag–Guneshli concession. Itochu's share was 20 percent of the NAOC (North Apsheron Operating Company) consortium developing the Asrafi–Dan–Ulduzu concession. Another trading company, Mitsui's affiliate, signed a basic document for joint development of the Kurdashi offshore block at the time of President Aliyev's visit to Japan in February 1998. Mitsui's 15 percent stake is combined with the 50 percent stake of SOCAR (State Oil Company of Azerbaijan), the 25 percent stake of Italy's Agip, and the smaller shares of Spain's Repsol and Turkey's TPAO. Moreover, a consortium of four Japanese companies—namely, Japan Petroleum Exploration Co. Ltd. (JAPEX), INPEX, Itochu, and Teikoku Oil Co. Ltd.—signed a contract with SOCAR for the development of a Caspian offshore oil field on the basis of a production-sharing arrangement (50 percent share) in December, 1998. Supported by Japan National Oil Corporation (JNOC), they established an operating company, Japan Azerbaijan Oil Co., Ltd. (JAOC), and started seismic exploration work in late 1999.

With regard to Kazakhstan, two geological survey projects in inland areas are being undertaken by three Japanese companies. The strong desire of Japanese companies to participate in actual oil development in the Kazakh sector of the North Caspian Sea materialized when it was agreed that a Japanese consortium led by INPEX would join the OKIOC (Offshore Kazakhstan International Operating Company) consortium composed of Agip, British Gas, BP Amoco, Statoil, ExxonMobil, Shell, and Total by acquiring half of the one-seventh share previously held by a Kazakh firm (KCS). The international consortium presently keeps twelve offshore blocks and is the group carrying out test drilling in the very promising Kashagan formation. The significance of the Japanese participation was underlined by the fact that President Nazarbayev attended the signing ceremony of the contract in September 1998 and expressed the hope that the agreement would facilitate the provision of yen credit and direct investment to Kazakhstan.

As for Turkmenistan, two Japanese firms were involved in the now-dormant international consortium initially led by Unocal to evaluate the possibility of a gas pipeline through Afghanistan to markets in Pakistan and, potentially, India. Mitsubishi is interested in a possible gas pipeline to China and is carrying out a feasibility study together with CNPC (China National Petroleum Company) and ExxonMobil.

Concerning gas and oil resource development in the Caspian Basin, one basic consideration in terms of energy security for Japan deserves special emphasis. For Asian countries, including Japan and China, Caspian oil and gas could serve the important objective of reducing through diversification their over-dependence on Persian Gulf and Middle East energy resources. While the United States shifts its major source of supply to Latin America away from the Middle East, Asian dependence on the Middle East is increasing in an alarming manner. From this point of view, Caspian oil and gas resources should not be channeled primarily through Iran and the Persian Gulf, and pipelines to the east to China would be most welcome. In addition to the idea noted above of a possible gas pipeline from Turkmenistan, how and to what extent Japan should cooperate in a possible oil pipeline from western Kazakhstan to China is an issue worthy of serious policy debate.

IV. EUROPE IN THE NEW CENTRAL ASIA

Alexander Rahr

The siege of Kazan in 1552 and the founding of Astrakhan in the Volga Delta in 1556 opened the road to European Russia's expansion into the Caucasus and Central Asia. That geographical expansion of Europe was continued in the 19th century in the course of the "Great Game" between two Europe-centered world empires—imperial Russia and imperial Britain.[1] For most Europeans, however, Central Asia and the Caucasus were never traditional areas of interest. With the re-conquest of Central Asia in the early years of the Soviet Union under the banner of the Bolshevik First Army headquartered at Ashkhabad, the mission "to set the East ablaze" was accomplished. But under Soviet Communism, Central Asia remained completely isolated from world politics. The area stayed far to the back of European minds until a new Central Asia appeared on the map after the breakup of the Soviet Union in 1991, composed of five newly independent states.

The European Union, aware that these states were not prepared to manage their newly gained independence and highly concerned this positive development could fail—leaving the area in limbo or, worse, reintegrating it under Russian control—declared that major efforts to stabilize these countries through assistance and other means had to be launched. But in contrast to the U.S. policy set out in chapter II, neither the governments of individual European states nor the European Union as a whole have, so far, developed a comprehensive agenda regarding this economically and politically fast-changing region.

Will Europe's long-standing tendency to see Central Asia through the prism of Russia change? It is clear that, after one decade of independence, the Central Asian states are disillusioned with the West. Expectations of joining the wider world with the assistance of the West have not materialized; they remain poor and isolated. This disillusionment with the West is leading the Central Asian states to search for external support from elsewhere; and their obvious and natural tendency is to look toward Russia, especially after the change of leadership in the Kremlin. President Putin has gladly accepted this opportunity and chose Central Asia for his first state visit abroad after his inauguration. He dished out many promises, primarily promises of support on security matters in an area where growing Islamic extremism is seen by the local regimes as the main threat to their survival. Europe remains aloof while recognizing at the same time that terrorism likewise threatens its own societies. For Europeans the most topical question is whether we should "engage" or "contain" Russia in the new Central Asia. Or will a united Europe acquire a different prism for looking at Central Asia in the 21st century?

A. EUROPE'S PRESENCE, EUROPE'S CONCERNS

How present is Europe today in the region? What should the concerns and ambitions of EU countries be at the beginning of the 21st century in the new Central Asia?

1. Europe's Presence

It is difficult to distinguish a common European approach. Each and every country pursues its own interests, be they commercial or political—not uncommon for other parts of the world as well. In most EU foreign ministries, Central Asia continues to be handled through the CIS department, which reinforces the Russian prism and tends to neglect the major influence of southern and eastern neighbors on developments in the area. The larger EU countries—most notably Germany—have opened diplomatic missions (see Table IV-1), often following major firms.

The European public cannot imagine the new Central Asian countries as applicants for either EU or NATO membership; nor do politicians and government officials. The lack of flight connections and tourist infrastructure also leave the region largely isolated from European public view. At the beginning of the 21st century, for the majority of European leaders and citizens, Central Asia remains a *terra incognito*.

The European business community is reluctant to promote the region as an emerging market for the 21st century, with the important exception of oil and gas companies. European energy companies have had a much longer presence in the area than their governments. A number of these firms were active in the area already in Soviet

TABLE IV-1
Europe's Diplomatic Representation in Central Asia: Germany, France, and the United Kingdom Compared to Japan and the United States
(number of resident diplomats)

	Germany	France	UK	Japan	USA
Kazakhstan	29	17	6	13	67
Kyrgyzstan	11	0	0	0*	22
Tajikistan	6	0	0	0	0
Turkmenistan	6	4	5	0	12
Uzbekistan	26	17	5	12	31
Total	78	38	16	25	132

Source: The Japan figures are from the Japanese Ministry of Foreign Affairs. The other figures are from the British Foreign and Commonwealth Office, as presented in House of Commons, Select Committee on Foreign Affairs, 1998–99 Session, Sixth Report, *South Caucasus and Central Asia* (London: 1999). See www.publications.parliament.uk/pa/cm199899/cmselect/cmfaff/349/34907 and 34914.

* Two Japanese with non-diplomatic status are posted at the Japan Center in Bishkek.

times—for example, Elf and Total, BP and Shell, Agip and Eni, Statoil and Petrofina. European energy firms have a strong presence in the international consortia now exploring for and developing oil and gas resources in the Caspian Basin. BP Amoco, for instance, is the lead company in the largest project so far in Azerbaijan, the AIOC (Azerbaijan International Operating Company) consortium developing the offshore Azeri–Chirag–Guneshli block. BP Amoco is also the leading company in the consortium which recently discovered very large gas deposits in the Shakh–Deniz block in the Azerbaijani sector of the Caspian Sea. Table IV-3 sets out the participants in a broad range of oil and gas ventures in Azerbaijan.

Trade has increased between Europe and Central Asia, albeit from a very low level. Since 1991, these countries have loosened formerly exclusive links to the Russian economy. Exports from the five Central Asian countries to the other successor republics of the USSR fell from 68 percent of total exports in 1992 to 41 percent in 1997. Imports from other successor republics fell from 66 percent to 50 percent within the same period of time. Table IV-2 presents EU15 trade with the five Central Asian countries and Azerbaijan in 1999, and indicates the limited scale of this trade from a European perspective (less than one-

TABLE IV-2
EU15 Trade with Central Asia and Azerbaijan, 1999
(millions of euros and as percent of global total)

	EU 15 Exports	EU 15 Imports	Balance
Kazakhstan	974.7	1,773.5	-798.8
Kyrgyzstan	76.4	130.9	-54.6
Tajikistan	32.3	54.9	-22.7
Turkmenistan	206.6	247.9	-41.3
Uzbekistan	497.3	392.6	+104.7
Azerbaijan	214.2	444.1	-229.9
Total	2,001.5	3,043.9	-1,042.5
As % of Global Total	0.26%	0.39%	

Source: Eurostat

half of one percent of total exports and total imports). Nevertheless, European countries have benefited the most from the diversification of Central Asia's trading links, enabling some European companies to see Central Asia as a growing market of 54 million consumers for their products. The Russian financial crisis, which struck in August 1998, had a strong negative impact on Central Asian economies and further enhanced the importance of Europe as a stable and reliable trading partner, although for many in the region, post-crisis Western aid was "too little and too late."

The involvement of the European Bank for Reconstruction and Development (EBRD) represents another dimension of Europe's presence. As of the end of 1998, the EBRD had disbursed about 450 million ecu to Central Asia and Azerbaijan, and committed almost 700 million more (see Table IV-4).

On top of flows from individual EU countries, Europe's presence is augmented by EU-level technical assistance programs for the new independent states of the former Soviet Union (TACIS), food aid, and humanitarian assistance. From 1992 through 1998, EU-level grant assistance totalled about 860 million ecus (see Table IV-5). Compared to ODA from the United States and Japan, Europe's flows are quite remarkable when member-state and EU-level aid are added together.

EU Partnership and Cooperation Agreements (PCAs) with the new independent states provide, for the first time, a common platform

Table IV-3
Energy Companies in Azerbaijan
(percentage stake in particular field)

	Absheron December 12, 1994	Ashrafi, Dan Ulduzu (oper. by NAOC) February 13, 1996	Azeri, Chirag, Gunashli (oper. by AIOC) October 17, 1996	Karabakh (oper. by CIPCO) February 25, 1997	Lankaran Talysh January 13, 1997	Nakhchivan January 13, 1997	Oguz August 1, 1997	Shakh-Deniz August 1, 1997	Kurdashi September, 1997	S. Gobustan June, 1998	Inam June,1998	Abikh (Araz, Alov, Sharg) July, 1998	Muradkhanli, Jafarli, Zardab July, 1998	Yalama	Kursangia, Karabagli
Est. Invest. ($ mil.)	2,500	1,500	8,000	2,000	2,000				2,000	800		4,000	1,000		
Azerbaijan															
SOCAR	50%	20%	10%	7.5%	25%	50%	50%	10%	50%	20%	50%	40%	50%	40%	50%
Europe-based															
Agip				5%					25%						
BP			17.13%					25.5%				15%			
Deminex					10%										
Elf					40%			10%							
Monument											12.5%				
Petrofina					5%										
Ramco			2.08%												
Repsol									5%				50%		
Statoil			8.56%					25.5%				15%			
Total	20%				10%										

US or Canada-based															
AEC												5%			
Amerada-Hess												15%			10%
Amoco		30%	17.01%								25%				
Chevron	30%														
Commonwealth										80%					
Exxon			8%			50%									
Frontera															30%
Mobil							50%								
Pennzoil			4.82%	30%											
Unocal		25.5%	10.05%												
Japan-based															
Itochu		20%	3.92%												
Mitsui									15%						
Others															
Central Fuel (Russia)											12.5%				
Delta (Saudi Arabia)		4.5%	1.68%												10%
LukAgip (Russia/Italy)				45%											
LukArco (Russia/US)														60%	
Lukoil (Russia)			10%	12.5%				10%							
OIEC (Iran)					10%			10%							
TPAO (Turkey)			6.75%					9%	5%			10%			
Grand Total	100%	100%	100%	100%	100%	100%	100%	100%	100%	100%	100%	100%	100%	100%	100%

Source: First Exchange Corporation, "Azerbaijan: Oil Companies: Who Is Doing What?" 19 May 1999, www.first-exchange.com/fsu/azer/plus/companies.htm.

Note: There has been some consolidation among the companies listed on this table. For instance, Exxon and Mobil have become ExxonMobil. BP and Amoco have become BP Amoco. Total, Petrofina, and Elf have combined into TotalFinaElf. Deminex has become VOG (Veba Oil and Gas). Shares in particular fields are bought and sold over time. For instance, Monument was acquired by Lasmo, which sold its stakes in the Inam field to Royal Dutch Shell.

from which to address political, economic, and other issues. These PCAs, which came into force with Kazakhstan, Uzbekistan, and Kyrgyzstan in the summer of 1999, specify that "respect for democracy, principles of international law and human rights as well as principles of market economy underpin the internal and external policies of the Parties and constitute a constant element of partnership." This explains why PCA negotiations with Turkmenistan, which has a particularly negative record on human rights, have been prolonged for another two years. PCAs are a "half-way house" between the standard framework agreements negotiated by the Commission with a number of countries worldwide and the "Europe Agreements" with the EU applicant countries. In July 2000 the EU held for the second time its Cooperation Council with Kazakhstan and Kyrgystan, and reiterated its willingness to cooperate closely with both countries. Europe's foreign ministers underlined that, as the European Union looks to enlarge, relations between it and Central Asia are set to assume greater importance. However, the political message which should be understood by the Central Asian countries is that, while European markets are being opened to them, they can not expect EU membership in any foreseeable future.

TABLE IV-4
EBRD Disbursements and Commitments
to Central Asia and Azerbaijan, as of End 1998
(millions of ecus)

	Disbursed	Committed (not yet disbursed)	Total
Kazakhstan	91.1	237.1	328.3
Kyrgyzstan	80.8	48.3	129.1
Tajikistan	2.1	10.8	12.9
Turkmenistan	27.4	94.9	122.3
Uzbekistan	146.3	207.0	353.3
Azerbaijan	98.6	94.0	192.5
Total	446.2	692.1	1138.3

Source: Based on EBRD Annual Report, Table 10 (Analysis of Operational Activity) as presented in House of Commons, Select Committee on Foreign Affairs, Sixth Report, 1998-99 Session, *South Caucasus and Central Asia* (London: 1999), www.publications.parliament.uk/pa/cm199899/cmselect/cmfaff/349/34913.htm.

In the TACIS framework, two well-known programs are the INOGATE (Interstate Oil and Gas Transport to Europe) and TRACECA (Transport Corridor Europe–Caucasus–Central Asia) projects. The EU is proud of these projects supporting the establishment of a proper transport infrastructure—a modern "Silk Road"—connecting the countries of the region to Europe as well as to each other. In July 1999, Romania, Bulgaria, and Ukraine joined the INOGATE umbrella agreement on the institutional framework for the establishment of oil and gas transportation systems. This indicates the potential importance of transport corridors to West European markets through Black Sea ports and a peaceful Balkans. Former EU Commissioner Hans van den Broek underlined that, through TRACECA and INOGATE, Europeans hope to play their part in bringing energy products and other goods through the ports of Odessa, Constanza, Varna, and Burgas to European markets.

But these energy and transport projects develop slowly—they are stuck in the feasibility studies stage—so the real impact on the economies of the new independent countries has yet to be felt. They require additional funding which is presently not available. INOGATE received in 1999 only 10 million euros and TRACECA 9

TABLE IV-5
EU-Level Grant Assistance to Central Asia and Azerbaijan, 1992–98
(millions of ecus)

	TACIS	Food and Humanitarian	Total Grants
Kazakhstan	111.6	0.0	111.6
Kyrgyzstan	52.2	82.2	134.5
Tajikistan	13.0	153.1	166.1
Turkmenistan	41.3	2.1	43.4
Uzbekistan	100.8	0.0	100.8
Azerbaijan	78.5	224.8	303.3
Total	397.4	462.2	859.7

Source: European Commission, as presented in House of Commons, Select Committee on Foreign Affairs, Sixth Report, 1998–99 Session, *South Caucasus and Central Asia,* Annex C (London: 1999).

* The Food and Humanitarian amounts for Azerbaijan and Tajikistan include some miscellaneous additional grant assistance (12.5 for Azerbaijan, 4.7 for Tajikistan).

million euros (out of a total of 31 million euros allocated to the TACIS inter-state programs).

The Energy Charter Treaty (ECT) which came into force in April 1998 is the first legal agreement for practical implementation of the principles laid down in the European Energy Charter of 1992 signed by fifty-two countries worldwide. The European Energy Charter's ambitions can only be fulfilled if both Russia and the United States—which have remained outside so far—participate fully in its implementation through the Energy Charter Treaty, calling for all states to take measures for facilitating the free and non-discriminatory transit of energy. In July 1999 a Transit Working Group was launched to prepare political negotiations for legally binding decisions to be completed by the end of 2000.

Central Asia's most serious problem is its dramatic social-economic decline since independence. The combined GDP of Azerbaijan, Kazakhstan, and Turkmenistan is now less than the GDP of the city of Bremen! More than half of the populations in the new Central Asia live below officially recognized poverty levels. The August 1998 financial crash in Russia worsened the poverty picture in Central Asia. Fostering stability in the area is obviously more difficult under

Beyond basic human needs, Europeans are concerned that other issues be addressed. "Good governance" is the catchword in this respect. Beyond bilateral and TACIS projects, Europe's assistance in this essential field is rendered through the Office of Democratic Institutions and Human Rights (ODIHR) of the OSCE, which participates in funding projects which address issues such as legislative reform, election standards, and civil society, along with other human rights projects. For example, 380 million ecus were allocated in 1998 to Kazakhstan, Kyrgystan, and Turkmenistan. The OSCE, in security affairs, has a very important early warning function and is expanding its capacities both at headquarters and in the field. The Council of Europe in Strasbourg also funds and implements various democracy-building projects in the Caucasus which should be extended now to Central Asia. (Georgia has been included as a member in the Council of Europe and will be followed shortly by Armenia and Azerbaijan.) Furthermore, European NGOs are present in the area. They are particularly focused on health care and education, seen as key elements of social infrastructure. (Medicins Sans Frontieres is practically alone operating in Tajikistan.) With all these programs in Central Asia, Europeans want to foster the emergence of strong local civil societies and stem the tide towards greater authoritarianism. As of today, the regimes of the new independent states in the southern tier of the former Soviet Union are largely characterized by aging leaders and energy-financed oligarchies ruling over increasingly alien societies. The European Union should expect from its new partners full respect for the basic human rights treaties they have ratified, without pressing these countries to copy Western European democratic models.

2. Europe's Concerns: Drugs, Terrorism, Immigration, Environment
In the first half of the nineties, Central Asia and its conflicts still appeared remote. But in the second half of the nineties, European societies became aware of huge problems emerging from this area which concern the lives of people in an immediate way—illegal immigration, drug trafficking, terrorism, growing criminality. These concerns are felt not only at the national level but also within the European institutions in Brussels.

EU member states agreed in February 2000 on an Action Plan aimed at combating drug traffic between the five Central Asia countries and the EU, building on a joint Franco–British anti-drug policy vis-à-vis Afghanistan. Afghanistan is now the world's largest heroin producer, and in this and other ways continues to destabilize Central Asian societies. International efforts to suppress the flow of drugs from Afghanistan to Central Asia have been a total failure; only 1.4 percent of estimated drug flows were intercepted in 1998! Europe's efforts so far have been criticized in Central Asia as being only rhetoric without serious funding. At the same time, Europe is expecting a far greater commitment by the local authorities to deal with drug flows more effectively. While the United States has committed billions of dollars this year to fight drug production and trafficking at the source in Colombia, the EU has not realized that Central Asia and Afghanistan merit similar efforts.

Increasing terrorism throughout Central Asia and the Caspian Basin, closely linked to drugs and often associated with radical Islamic groups, is a challenge with which the European Union will have to cope if it seriously cares about stability in the region. (Islam is now Europe's second religion.) Uzbekistan and Kazakhstan proposed at the November 1999 OSCE Istanbul Summit a greater fight against terrorism, particularly through the setting up of an international anti-terrorist center in Tashkent, which should be welcomed. Another center for combating terrorism was created within the CIS in June

2000 (without the participation of Turkmenistan). It is deplorable that this issue of global importance and particular topicality to the stability of Central Asia was disregarded at the recent G-8 Okinawa Summit. Anti-terrorism efforts, the focus of a special summit in Sharm-el-Sheik in the nineties, must surely remain of central concern to G-8 leaders in the coming years.

Demographic change, migration pressures, and refugee flows are another cluster of key concerns. In the long term, major population growth in South Asia, Iran, and China is likely to impact Central Asia, its resources, and its societies, and in turn affect Russia. In a nearer timeframe, migration and population displacements can create insecurity, heighten ethnic tensions, and undermine an already fragile social order. (At the end of 1999, the number of refugees and other persons of concern to UNHCR in Central Asia was 875,000.) Of great relevance to Europeans is the number of asylum-seekers originating from Central Asia, which has increased dramatically since the end of 1999. Europe must therefore be concerned.

In a context of dramatic population movements, Central Asian environmental issues are likely to become even larger challenges, challenges which may one day threaten Europe. Examples are water issues, including the drying up of the Aral Sea, and nuclear cleanup issues, including at the former Soviet nuclear testing site in Semipalatinsk.

These issues are so close to the daily concerns of European citizens that they must lead to the new Central Asia being put higher on the agenda of national politicians. Indeed, the EU's "Third Pillar"—cooperation on home and justice affairs and in the struggle against crime, corruption, terrorism, and drug trafficking—could become a major basis for dealing with Central Asia and the Caucasus.

B. DEVELOPING EUROPE'S POLITICAL STRATEGY: GIVING SUBSTANCE TO THE COMMON FOREIGN AND SECURITY POLICY

Third Pillar issues could thus become the stepping stones toward a more ambitious and comprehensive European political strategy towards Central Asia. So far European political leaders lack a political vision for that geographically remote region. Many decision-makers in the EU consider the non-existence of such a "strategy" correct, as any approach to these countries should be purely grounded in economic and certainly not geostrategic considerations. For instance, the EU, it is said, does not favor fixing political values to pipeline routes, contrary to other players in the region. But should the EU remain only an economic contributor to regional stability and accept that its economic might is to be exploited politically by other actors?

So far, the EU countries have not found a common denominator for engagement in that part of the world. For this to change, a large country probably needs to lead the process. However, Germany, the largest exporter to the area, has no major oil and gas companies there. France, Great Britain, and Italy are home countries of leading companies involved in finding oil and gas around the Caspian Sea and could engineer the harmonization of European strategic interests with more political credibility. But finding oil and gas is not the big issue in the new "Great Game" in the region. The real geopolitical competition is centered on pipeline routes, a competition that requires a stronger political engagement from the EU.

In October 1999, the European Union, in accordance with the Amsterdam Treaty, formally started to develop its "Common Foreign and Security Policy" (CFSP). Future European strategic planning will focus on potential crisis areas, with a particular focus on civil emergency planning. The region stretching from the Balkans and the Black Sea through the Caucasus and Central Asia to the border of China will surely become, within the next decade, an area where the High Representative for CFSP will wish to establish the EU as an international actor in its own right. A first step was undertaken with the joint EU–Caucasus Summit in June 1999 in Luxembourg, and proposals are in circulation for a "Stability Pact" for the Caucasus.

The governments of the EU countries needed ten years after the tearing down of the Iron Curtain in Europe to accept the Balkans as part of their security zone. Another decade will probably be required before EU governments start regarding the Caspian region or Central Asia as within their sphere of security interests. The new independent states along the southern tier of the former Soviet Union could face problems similar to those in the Balkans. Conflicts in the region could quickly develop, with direct consequences for European societies. Western military engagement in the Yugoslav crisis aimed to halt civil war, to forestall massive emigration to Western Europe, and to build democracy. Compared to the former Yugoslavia, a serious crisis in the Caucasus or Central Asia will add another crucial dimension to the agenda for intervention: energy security. It would also immediately involve a range of other regional powers that regard Central Asia and the Caucasus as part of their security zones. Europe needs to clarify its policies toward

these other regional powers—Iran, Turkey, China, not to mention
Russia—policies that may conflict with those of the United States.

A few basic questions need to be more thoroughly addressed by
the EU countries and their High Representative for CFSP:

- What are the instruments for an ambitious EU policy in the Caspian
  and Central Asia?

- What should a joint EU strategy for the region include? How would
  it differ from U.S. strategy? Could serious tensions with the United
  States emerge over Central Asia and the Caspian Basin?

- Is a "Stability Pact" like the one for Southeast Europe feasible for
  the Caucasus or Central Asia? How can such an effort become more
  than a "bag of ingeniously cooked fudge"?[2]

After the breakup of the Soviet Union, all successor states of the
former USSR automatically became members of the CSCE. The
leading industrial states of the West—the founding fathers of that
organization together with the Soviet Union in the mid-
seventies—thereby took some measure of responsibility for
supporting the new independent states on their path towards
democracy and a market economy. It was considered that these states
should remain harnessed to Euro-Atlantic institutions. The Paris
Charter of 1990 mentioned Central Asia as an area of all-European
security interest. The CSCE (renamed OSCE at the December 1994
Budapest Summit) managed to establish its "missions" and liaison
offices in Central Asia and the Caucasus. It provided the legal
framework for subsequent peacekeeping operations involving both
Russian troops and Western observers.

NATO, a much more powerful and effective organization,
designed a special program—the Partnership for Peace—for countries
which had just escaped Soviet rule. The majority of Caucasus and
Central Asian states joined this program, albeit with limited success.
One problem was that the Central Asian defense ministries
implementing these programs at the technical level came into conflict
with their foreign ministry colleagues, the former still looking to
Moscow while the latter were turning increasingly to Brussels.
During NATO's Kosovo bombing campaign, the Central Asian
military leaderships were influenced by their Russian counterparts
and relations cooled between them and NATO. Since the end of the
war, however, relations have become warmer again, as exemplified by
the NATO Secretary General's recent visit to the area. Of particular
interest was George Robertson's stressing that building closer

relations with NATO by these countries would not damage their relationship with Russia. Nevertheless, some in NATO quarters talk cautiously of "failed partners." Military cooperation in the framework of Partnership for Peace has clearly reached its limits, and the NATO program is in the midst of serious reappraisal. The focus of NATO's military planners has switched from a broader OSCE framework to a narrower Balkan perspective.

Individual states of the region have progressed differently in building their ties with Europe. Georgia, Armenia, and Azerbaijan have been admitted to the Council of Europe. Geography compels the Caucasus states to draw closer to NATO, while the Central Asians are more interested in economic links with the EU. As mentioned earlier, Kazakhstan, Uzbekistan, and Kyrgyzstan (but not Turkmenistan and Tajikistan) have signed "Partnership and Cooperation Agreements" (PCAs) with the EU.

Like NATO, the EU is reviewing its "instruments" for dealing with Central Asian and Caspian countries. But tools without a design are ineffectual: A more clear-cut vision in dealing with Central Asia and the Caucasus is urgently required. Bureaucratic hurdles exist within the European institutions, particularly between the Commission and the Council. The Commission is reluctant to hand over its operational tools in foreign affairs to the Council. On the other hand, the Commission has developed concrete proposals with the necessary financing for a comprehensive EU policy towards the Caspian region, but these proposals have been ignored by the Council, which argues that too many uncertainties prevail in the area. For the Council, European involvement in the region is primarily the responsibility of the business community. Such turf warfare between the European Commission and the European Council disrupts the building of a common European strategy.

Europe's strategic goal for the region has to be stability. Helsinki-type confidence-building measures (CBMs) will be useful instruments. This should include setting up regular, inclusive "Round Tables" involving politicians, business leaders, and experts on the main issues related to stability in the area, including Islam's future role. The Minsk Group on Nagorno-Karabakh is not effective, partly because the United States and Russia have their own hidden agendas on Armenia. The OSCE has been only partly effective, with the exception of its High Commissioner for National Minorities, who has helped to diffuse tensions in a politically highly charged area. The just-established Rapid Response Team (REACT) under the new

Istanbul OSCE Charter for European Security should show its utility by rapidly deploying civilian and police experts to the area. Unfortunately, bureaucratic hurdles and a general lack of funds are obstructing its implementation.

Over the past decade, the EU has attempted to play a role in the former Soviet South through economic assistance, with a particular emphasis on building intra-regional cooperation structures through the TRACECA and INOGATE projects noted above. Through these structures, the EU hopes to hasten economic recovery and thus help dampen existing inter-ethnic and territorial conflicts. But so far the benefits of aid (and foreign investment) have gone largely to the oligarchs—the former Soviet ruling elites now governing these new states. The danger exists that oil and other revenues will be used for an arms buildup and further destabilize a volatile region. Through bilateral military contacts and cooperation agreements that already exist between European countries and the Central Asians, monitoring mechanisms should be explored which would discourage an arms build-up.

Other challenges for European engagement in the region (sometimes shared by Japan) arise from differences with Europe's major ally, the United States:

- Europe differs with the United States regarding containment of Iran. Most European governments do not accept the U.S. notion of "rogue states" (since re-labelled "states of concern"). In fact, they regard Iran as a key future partner in commercial operations in the Caspian region. This explains Europe's "constructive dialogue" policy with Iran launched a few years ago and enhanced more recently after the encouraging results of Iran's parliamentary elections. President Mohammad Khatami recently visited France and Germany. Iran also facilitates rapprochement with Europe by supporting Europe's struggle against drug-trafficking.

- Although Europeans basically share the U.S. policy of strengthening the independence of the new states in the former Soviet South through diversifying their links with the wider world, Europeans are more eager than Americans to give Russia a major role in the pipeline network around the Caspian Basin and to give Russia's oil companies a greater presence in the consortia operating in the area. Engaging Russia in all aspects of European economic and security policy remains part of the paradigm for the EU's common foreign and security policy, even more so after the election of President Putin. Moreover, from the European perspective, Russia is the bulwark against the various challenges emanating from Central Asia and the

Caucasus for Europe. However, questions can be raised as to the way Moscow performs this difficult task; Chechnya is a case in point.

- Major states of the EU have embarked on bilateral military-technological cooperation with individual states of the former Soviet South. But they remain reluctant to use NATO's Partnership for Peace Program for any kind of anti-Russian maneuvering in the region. In contrast to the United States, the EU states would like Russia to strengthen its peacekeeping role in the area. It is unfortunate that European Union states, who today deplore the loss of influence of the OSCE, did not seize the opportunity in 1993 to play the role offered to them by Russia in the Nagorno-Karabakh conflict. The double containment of Russia to the north and Iran to the south that is high on the U.S. strategic agenda is in contradiction with the more cooperative and longer-term path that the EU wishes to pursue in the region with Russia and Iran.

- Also, the EU does not share the U.S. fascination with Turkey as the key Central Asian and Caucasus anchor. Europeans see the danger of Turkey becoming too much used to contain Iran and Russia. The second Chechen War and President Putin's trips to Central Asia were interpreted in Turkey as attempts by the new Russian President to revive the former "empire." The EU does not support the U.S. vision of Turkey as the main transport country for oil and gas to Western markets, while acknowledging at the same time the necessity to reduce the heavy tanker traffic through the Bosporus. A case in point is the Baku–Ceyhan oil pipeline strongly supported by the United States government. The EU is taking a broader approach to pipeline diplomacy. Its Caspian pipeline strategy includes routes to Europe through Romania and Bulgaria (both EU applicant countries) and Ukraine.

- The Europeans cautiously express the fear that a domineering U.S. policy in the region could, in the long run, provoke the kind of "Great Game" balance-of-power competition which the Trilateral countries want to avoid. The EU fears the setting-up of new "blocs" in the region—for example a US–Turkey–GUUAM bloc versus a Russia–Iran–Armenia or even a Russia–China–Central Asia bloc (in the form of the "Shanghai Five," renamed the "Shanghai Forum" in July 2000). Even more cautiously, some European decision-makers are beginning to argue that the EU has a political role to play in the region as a mediator should a serious conflict break out between the United States and Russia or China.

C. A "STABILITY PLAN" FOR THE REGION?

Different plans for the Caspian region are on the table. The EU approach (based on the EU–Caucasus Luxembourg Summit in 1999 and influenced by the second Russian war in Chechnya and the current fighting between government forces and Islamic militants in Central Asia) gives top priority to engagement of all key actors, including those involved in the commercial exploitation of Caspian Basin resources. Joint peacekeeping operations under OSCE mandate throughout the region—an idea put forward by Russia in 1993—should be the next step of an EU strategy. The EU will continue to support with the regional actors any plans that combat terrorism and drug-trafficking and that seek to avoid lawlessness such as in Chechnya. EU thinking may possibly materialize in a comprehensive Action Plan on the model of the Balkan Stability Pact, with the German Foreign Ministry as the architect.

A different "stability plan" for the Caucasus was developed by former President Süleyman Demirel of Turkey. He wants to embrace Georgia and Azerbaijan—and maybe even Armenia—in an economic and security alliance, which could then expand towards Central Asia. The Turkish plan explicitly ignores Russia and Iran. Since the December 1999 EU Helsinki Summit gave Turkey the status of an EU applicant country, it is now very important for this country to discuss any further steps in the Caspian region more closely with Brussels and its High Representative, in order to avoid misunderstandings or discrepancies.

Russia's new President Vladimir Putin has also put forward a "stability plan" for Central Asia, which he restated at the G-8 Summit in Okinawa. Russia's recent military conquest in Chechnya seems to imply closer integration with the Caucasus and Central Asia under the banner of fighting Islamic terrorism. Putin's plan is rooted in Russia's new foreign political and military "doctrine" of resisting U.S. unilateralism and favoring a multipolar world. Here Russian concerns come close to Chinese and, increasingly, West European concerns. Russia's fear of expulsion from its former South, including from economic relations, also fuels Putin's view of the area, exemplified in his October 1999 strategy document submitted to EU countries. These considerations need to be taken into account in Europe's general policy vis-à-vis this major player. One example of Putin's new approach is the appointment of a Special Representative in charge of coordinating Moscow's policy towards the states around the Caspian Sea and mellowing Russia's previously heavy-handed pipeline policy.

The success of any "stability plan" depends on whether it can solve the existing territorial and ethnic conflicts, help restore the ailing economies of the new independent states in the region, and deliver long-lasting security arrangements. The various plans overlap in ways that waste political energy and scarce financial resources in the quest for stability that remains the common thread through these different initiatives.

Coordination mechanisms between various institutions involved in Central Asian issues need to be created. Finding common ground should not be too difficult but actually committing the necessary funds is likely to be another story (as shown by the experience of the Stability Pact for the Balkans, where the EU, by raising false expectations, has provoked an anti-Western backlash in the region which requires urgent mending). Although the EU's High Representative would be suitable for this coordinating role, it would be more politically correct for a strengthened OSCE to undertake this task.

Noted above was the EU emphasis on the creation of a modern Silk Road. A modern Silk Road could, in the coming decades, run from the Balkans and the Black Sea though the Caucasus and Central Asia to China and Japan. It would open the new independent states to the outside world and promote business investment. It should also bring wide-ranging political benefits, moderating fears of a "clash of civilizations" in this part of the "arc of crises," and engaging Russia and other difficult neighbors economically and peacefully in a common design.

Europe's postwar history shows ways in which pooling economic tools can advance regional cooperation and peace. The European Coal and Steel Community (ECSC) set up in 1952 may be a particularly relevant example. One of Central Asia's most serious concerns is its limited water resources. A High Authority on Central Asian Water—on the model of the High Authority of the ECSC—could be a first step in creating a much-needed regional cooperative framework. This High Authority could be meshed into a broader regional economic strategy in the framework of the existing Central Asia Economic Union (CAEU). That organization, created in 1994, is composed of four Central Asian countries (in 1999 Turkmenistan, Ukraine, and Georgia joined as observers). A new commitment to regional cooperation and multilateralism was shown by the Central Asian leaders at their recent summit meeting. This should encourage the EU to build a closer relationship with the CAEU.

A prerequisite for stability in the region is a resolution of the Afghan civil war with its pernicious impact on Central Asia. Central Asian governments talk of "Islamic terrorism," as do many officials in Moscow. Particularly while Afghanistan remains a running sore, authoritative sources in Central Asia speak openly about the inevitability of a future war against Islamic forces. As this chapter was being completed in August 2000, there was an increase in deadly clashes between insurgents and government forces. The outcome of this fighting over time will be determined to a large extent by the support the insurgents find in troubled societies. Islam in more moderate forms will be an essential aspect of successful Central Asian societies over time and needs to be positively nurtured. The EU should advise the local authorities to follow the European example of incorporating peaceful and socially-oriented traditions within Islam into new civil society networks at the grassroots level.

V. CONCLUSIONS AND RECOMMENDATIONS

A new Central Asia is emerging, one that will reflect its Soviet past for decades to come, but cannot return to it. The region is slowly but surely becoming part of the wider world. The crucial questions are how this process will proceed and whether it will be defined for both the region and the outside world by its costs or by its benefits.

Over time, this new Central Asia will be linked to the wider world through air, land, and rail routes, as well as oil and gas pipelines. It will be linked by common cultural ties, but also divided—perhaps violently—by them. It may also be linked to the wider world by the narcotics trafficker, the terrorist, and the refugee. For some time to come, these Central Asian countries will be characterized by weak states, weak economies, and weak civil societies. They will be seeking some form of return to the Islamic world, though its form remains murky. The outcome of these trends could well be very different for each state. Russia will continue to play an important role, but, even with an energetic president and better economic times, it will no longer be the sole or dominant power. The new Central Asia will be part of a highly differentiated geopolitical space, with China, Iran, Turkey, Pakistan, and India interested and engaged.

While the direct impact of these potential internal and external developments for Trilateral countries may in the near term be slight, their indirect impact could be profound and will increase over time. As parts of this region become integrated into the wider world, Trilateral stakes will grow. The region will have a profound impact on Russian and Chinese stability, identity, and interests in the coming century. The Central Asian region will also be a force in shaping the interests, ambitions, and capabilities of states such as India, Iran, and Turkey. Regional conflicts could draw in outside powers and thus exacerbate larger Eurasian tensions. Such conflicts could also spill over into adjacent regions of primary significance to Trilateral countries, such as the Persian Gulf.

The Trilateral states could well play a decisive role in this region as a force for economic opportunity, global integration, and stability. The Trilateral states could do so precisely because none sees this region as a zone of vital interests. Trilateral energy companies seek to develop the region's oil and gas. Trilateral governments want these countries to cultivate economic reform, a moderate and open Islamic culture, and the political pluralism that is the engine for both. Yet no Trilateral state will make this region an area of primary focus. The derivative importance of this region is a great advantage in defining Trilateral policies for a regional "engagement without confrontation." However, this derivative importance could also rob policies of their fiscal and political momentum, turning them into empty rhetoric and squandering the influence Trilateral states now enjoy.

A. ELEMENTS OF A COMMON APPROACH

The overriding concern for Trilateral countries in this region has to be stability. The costs are high in the long run if weak states, corrupt gangs in and outside government, ethnic tensions, and outside aggressors make the region an exporter of tension and instability, rather than oil and gas. Stability in this context does not mean acquiescence to the status quo, but neither does it mean ignoring the new Central Asia's existing political and economic structures. The best overall policy is one of consistent and purposeful engagement with the region over an extended period. Such a policy has to begin with helping to address the region's pressing social needs and to relate the development of oil, gas, and other natural resource wealth to broad-based economic progress.

A lack of vital interests in the region could tempt Trilateral policies to one of two unwelcome extremes: The first is an "oil and gas only"policy, one willing to sacrifice the region's long-term economic and political improvement for short-run deals with the current regimes; the second is an abstract and unengaged preaching to states and societies in crisis of the virtues of Trilateral political forms and markets. Neither the cynicism of the first course nor the self-righteousness of the second is likely to lead to a better outcome for the region.

The first task for Trilateral decision-makers is to be wary of imposing a false unity on this part of the world. It is not a single region. While broadly Islamic, the countries of the region are not of a single ethnic, cultural, or religious tradition. Energy development will be a key economic factor for many, but not for all. Kyrgyzstan, Tajikistan, and Uzbekistan are not rich in energy resources for world markets, though long-term development of energy infrastructure in the broad region may make development of Uzbekistan's modest reserves commercially viable in 20–30 years. Weaknesses of state and civil society are widespread, but they are in fact forces for continuing decline and differentiation, not regional unity. Only Kyrgyzstan has managed to combine relative stability with an element of democracy. The others are differentiated by the age and vigor of their chief executive, geography, and economic prospects.

The expansion of political, commercial, and security ties with the outside world will bring further differentiation, as individual countries and sub-regions interact with China, Iran, Turkey, and other Eurasian states. Geography, internal and external factors, and other circumstances will incline some states toward China and others toward Iran, Turkey, or even India. The resulting pattern of relations, as they mature, will add complexity and variation to an already diverse region.

Russia will remain a key player but no longer the region's destiny. New energetic leadership in Moscow could make a great difference in the role Russia plays, as will Moscow's definition of its vital interests. A Russia that understands the growing multipolarity in the region and attempts to be an active partner with states in and outside the region will be far more influential than a Russia seeking to be the region's ruler or spoiler. Of these latter two roles, Russia's military, economic, and political resources—even with Putin and a stronger economy—are much more suited to the spoiler.

Trilateral strategic planning needs to expect highly differentiated internal development and external interactions. One could easily imagine this region becoming a mixture of internal successes and failures, as well as splitting into two or three distinct economic and geopolitical sub-regions. None of our shorthand labels for the countries capture this dynamism.

Each of the Trilateral states needs to examine its internal analytical and policy structures to make sure they reflect the region's dynamism. Those who place these countries unthinkingly in the bosom of the former Soviet Union are likely to miss the impact of China and of the Islamic world.

Given limitations on the amount of Trilateral assistance likely to be forthcoming, greater coordination and targeting of that assistance is essential. Trilateral policy-makers and providers of assistance have to increase their efforts to form a common understanding of the strategic stakes and a shared list of priorities. Natural affinities of one Trilateral state for a particular country, region or project ought to be encouraged. That assistance has to focus on pressing social needs, such as education and literacy and the decline in healthcare. These projects offer immediate assistance to the region and cast Trilateral engagement on the side of long-term social and economic improvements.

Trilateral states have to come to terms with the rise of new actors in the region. The new states themselves, no longer so new, have to be active partners in Trilateral policies. So do key rim countries, including Russia, China, Turkey, and Iran. Some of the possible combinations make for strange bedfellows, especially for those used to thinking in terms of either European or East Asian institutions and alliances. Yet the Trilateral presence could well soften the rough edges of those regional combinations now emerging, create real incentives for cooperation, and discourage the emergence of more dangerous regional rivalries.

Especially given the encouraging signs of political and social change in Iran, Trilateral countries have to see this important state as one of the keys to the region's future. Energy and transportation dilemmas ultimately require an Iranian contribution. The destabilizing elements associated with Iran—its terrorists and militants—have been much less present in Central Asia than in the Middle East. Though terrorism and proliferation concerns delay a fully normalized engagement with Tehran, they do not justify Iran's continued isolation, particularly given an emerging reform movement within the country. It makes little sense to exclude more constructive Iranian business, social, and cultural actors from Trilateral planning for the region.

B. ADDRESSING INTERNAL SOURCES OF INSTABILITY

The immense human, societal, and governmental needs of the region also create opportunities for greater Trilateral cooperation and for broad-based efforts that include Russia, China, and partners from the Islamic world. The shocking decline in public health and education, the decay or even absence of basic transportation and other social infrastructure, and the emergence of a wide range of religious and social organizations create targets for Trilateral assistance. A broad range of public health, rural development, and civil society programs would both meet real needs and foster a lasting link between Trilateral countries and the populations of these emerging states.

- Trilateral sponsors need to be realistic. These programs will not lead to swift democratization, but they could have an important influence on sustaining and broadening elements of pluralism that are a key to a more democratic future. Human rights cannot be forgotten, but they have to be embedded in a long-range strategy for raising the states of the region to world standards.

- Trilateral support of democracy needs to be long-term and tempered by realistic near-term expectations. Trilateral assistance has to focus on sources of peaceful pluralism in these states and societies. Inevitably, engagement of these sources brings Trilateral policies into a closer and much healthier encounter with Islam.

- Trilateral energy companies, governments, and international financial institutions need to consider ways to encourage the use of energy wealth to create the foundations for broad-based long-term economic growth and to address looming social problems. Powerful carrots and sticks are available to encourage restructuring and privatization. The often-neglected agricultural sector deserves major attention in this regard. For instance, private land ownership by farmers, combined with the availability of credit and protected by the court system, will be critical for rural economic progress.

- Trilateral assistance should include a focus on appalling health risks, such as tuberculosis or environmental degradation. The crushing poverty and lack of economic opportunity in many parts of the region make environmental and social concerns a low priority, even for those most affected by pollution and disease. Yet, left unattended, environmental and health issues will take their human toll and undermine economic development.

- Individual Trilateral states should continue to develop special partnerships with particular countries in the region, much like Canada has taken on special responsibility for Ukraine within the G-7. Japan, for example, has made special efforts in both Kyrgyzstan and Tajikistan. Such special partnerships could be another way of ensuring the assistance provided the region is well-targeted.

- Expanded anti-drug efforts are needed, for this area will continue to expand its contribution to the illegal drug trade. Trilateral countries should encourage and expand Interpol cooperation on drug trafficking, nuclear smuggling, and terrorism.

- The necessary focus on worst cases or areas where energy and geopolitical stakes are greatest should not lead Trilateral states to forget Kyrgyzstan. This country's success in pursuing market reforms and political pluralism, though still fragile, is impressive and deserves Trilateral support.

C. HEADING OFF REGIONAL RIVALRIES

Though many Russian observers see Trilateral, particularly U.S. and NATO, policies as aimed at supplanting Moscow, both the range and intensity of NATO's security cooperation effort fall far short of any active competition. In fact, on security matters, Trilateral policies, particularly U.S. and NATO Partnership for Peace efforts, have actively sought Russian cooperation. Russian military involvement in the region, the holdover of neo-imperial attitudes, and a decided decline in Moscow's influence there create enormous challenges for Russian policy, as well as resentment of outside actors.

However, if a core security problem for both Russia and the Trilateral countries in the near term is the stability of still weak states in the former USSR, a substantial basis for security cooperation exists. Stabilizing Russia's weak neighbors ought to be a core element of Trilateral policies toward Russia, for a weak and unstable neighborhood will present distractions, challenges, and temptations to a still weak and changing Russia. Ensuring that China's engagement in the region continues to be a stabilizing force is also a priority.

- The authors of this study agree that NATO has assumed a visibility in the region out of keeping with its real influence there. The new Central Asia is not a Euro- or Euro-Atlantic region but an inner Asian one. There should be no attempt to shut NATO out of the region. NATO's Partnership for Peace offers some of the best-funded and most successful military-to-military programs in the world. Yet NATO activism in the region might easily be misunderstood or deliberately distorted to harm Trilateral interests. This activism has also raised unrealistic expectations in the region of U.S. and NATO support in future crises, support that is unlikely to be forthcoming.

- Over time, Trilateral efforts have to focus on blending security cooperation with emerging regional security patterns and institutions. The region as a whole knows few successful multilateral security arrangements. CIS and Tashkent Treaty structures have gradually eroded, leaving Russia to attempt to salvage its influence through a set of bilateral agreements. However, the so-called Shanghai process, one bringing together Russia, China, Kazakhstan, Kyrgyzstan, and Tajikistan, has agreed on a range of ambitious confidence-building measures and troop and equipment reductions along the old Sino-Soviet border. This same group of states is making progress on settling long-standing border issues. The ECO and Turkic Summits are examples of emerging and not entirely successful

Islamically-oriented diplomacy. There is clearly room for new combinations, particularly those likely to promote greater security cooperation, openness, and conflict resolution. Both the G-7 and the G-8 could play a larger role here.

- Specifically, Trilateral countries should support the formation of a Central Asian Roundtable as a means to encourage senior-level dialogue between Trilateral countries (including Korea), states of the region, and key neighbors like China, Russia, Turkey, and Iran. Such a roundtable could be built around senior leaders in the region, like Presidents Karimov and Nazarbayev, and serve as an encouragement of transparency and cooperation on political, economic, and security assistance, as well as provide a more solid framework for addressing regional conflicts. Broad multilateral organizations with important roles in the area—the United Nations and UNDP, the World Bank and IMF, the ADB and EBRD—should also be part of this senior-level dialogue.

- The multilateral and cooperative mechanisms created to address Ukrainian denuclearization and Baltic troop withdrawals are models that ought to be applied to these new problems. There has to be some Trilateral support for internationalizing and ultimately resolving existing conflicts in the region. While no one expects NATO or Trilateral contingents of peacekeepers, it is clear that the region's conflicts are frozen, not resolved. And no resolution will be forthcoming if left to the parties on the ground. Trilateral policies should seek to strengthen the roles of the UN and, where appropriate, the OSCE. The United Nations (through UNMOT) and the OSCE jointly observed the 2000 elections in Tajikistan. Trilateral policies should promote an active effort to normalize Russian-dominated peacekeeping efforts and bring them into line with international standards of openness and operations.

- Afghanistan is a running sore. The settlement in Tajikistan will never take hold as long as its neighbor is in turmoil, while other states of the new Central Asia fear the long-term implications of Taliban control or further disintegration. Afghanistan is a major source of illegal drugs, fundamentalist militants, terrorists, and other forces of erosion of Central Asian stability. Trilateral countries have to develop an integrated and more serious strategy for addressing the Afghan situation and its regional implications. The first practical fruits of this strategy could well be increased assistance to regional anti-terrorism and anti-drug efforts and technical help in strengthening border controls.

- Trilateral countries ought to provide some basic security assistance, particularly that focused on border security, military reform, and long-term integration into multilateral operations. This assistance should be transparent and inclusive, where possible, of multiple regional players and neighboring states.

D. A LONG-TERM ENERGY STRATEGY

Energy resources can divide or unite the region. Properly developed, they make internal recovery more likely. However, they could also be the source of continued corruption and economic decline. The authors of this study believe that energy development, including the important goal of pipeline diversification, is and should be primarily an economic matter. However, the geopolitical aspects of these issues cannot be ignored.

- Trilateral governments should be active supporters of multiple pipelines. This will include upgraded new lines across Russian territory, such as the major oil pipeline being built by the Caspian Pipeline Consortium from Tengiz to Novorossiisk. It will also include non-Russian routes. The Baku–Supsa oil line is already in operation. The Baku–Ceyhan line, a major proposed oil pipeline, is not yet as economically attractive to Trilateral financiers and energy companies as it is geopolitically interesting to some Trilateral governments. Pipeline routes to or through Iran, for which there is strong commercial logic, should not be ruled out. In the long run, an eastern gas route from Turkmenistan should be welcomed, given rising East and South Asian energy demand. Over time the key to ensuring pipeline diversification is economic viability. The likely energy reserves of the region combined with healthy market forces should support this outcome.

- To the extent possible, the partnerships formed by Trilateral energy companies to develop energy resources from the new Central Asia ought to include Russian and Chinese energy firms. Trilateral policies should likewise encourage broad-based cooperation on pipeline development and security. A strong dose of economic com-petition and cooperation is the exact antidote needed for those who see the region only through the prism of geopolitical rivalry and a new "Great Game." Trilateral countries have an interest in seeing growth in the number and influence of Russian stakeholders in Central Asian energy development. There are encouraging signs that the Putin Administration is beginning to understand what Russia has to lose if it tries to be the spoiler of energy development in the region. Its own energy potential in the north Caspian and the need for enormous financial and technical resources to develop any major field in the area should also be a spur to strategic cooperation among Russian and selected Trilateral firms.

- Energy and a wide range of other concerns come together in proposals for a new "Silk Road" through Central Asia linking it to both Europe and East Asia. Links within the region and to Europe are being developed in the TRACECA and INOGATE projects sponsored by the EU, projects which deserve much more active support by the EU countries and their Trilateral partners. The development of links to China and on to Korea and Japan should also be of broad international interest.

- There also should be a broad and bold refashioning of the partnership between Trilateral governments and their private sector energy companies in the region. Energy development in the region is both a key to future economic prosperity for many states of the region and, if mishandled, a source of long-term political instability and economic decline. Trilateral government–private sector cooperation is necessary to help coordinate efforts and maximize leverage to encourage a positive economic and social outcome from the development of energy wealth. Trilateral governments should also work to ensure the policies of international financial institutions encourage such an outcome.

E. CONCLUSION

These policies seriously pursued are not the be-all and end-all for the new Central Asia. This region's future is in local, not Trilateral, hands. But Trilateral policies can make a difference in hastening the process of the region's political and economic integration with the wider world. They can contribute to the emergence of cooperative patterns and mechanisms of interstate relations. They can help bring about a solid economic foundation for long-term prosperity and a reversal of trends that threaten economic and societal decline. No short-term vital interest compels such a Trilateral approach to the region, but long-term trends in the region make it a prudent and inexpensive option. The authors of this study hope that Trilateral governments will see this opportunity to promote long-term stability and positive change in the new Central Asia and take it.

NOTES

Chapter I: Introduction

1.   Terry Koonce, "Caspian Energy Infrastructures: Past, Present, & Future," *The Cyber-Caravan*, 18 February 1998. Mr. Koonce was at the time President of Exxon Ventures (CIS) Inc. *The Cyber-Caravan* is an online publication of the Central Asia-Caucasus Institute in Washington, D.C., www.cacianalyst.org.

2.   Hilary McCutcheon and Richard Olson, "Risk Management, Financing Availability Keys to Winning in Caspian Region," *Oil & Gas Journal*, 24 July 2000, and Hilary McCutcheon and Richard Olson, "Coming to Terms with Risk in Caspian Region Yields More Realistic Production, Investment Outlook," *Oil & Gas Journal*, 21 August 2000. McCutcheon and Olson work for Wood Mackenzie. This Edinburgh-based consulting firm, a subsidiary of Deutsche Bank, carried out a study of the upstream Caspian Sea region. The Wood Mackenzie analysis excluded the Russian and Iranian sectors of the Caspian. Earlier this year Lukoil announced a discovery in the Russian sector estimated at about 2 billion barrels.

3.   Koonce, op. cit.

4.   Ibid.

5.   J. Robinson West and Julia Nanay, "Caspian Sea Infrastructure Projects," *Middle East Policy*, VII, no. 3 (2000): 114. Mr. West is Chairman of the Petroleum Finance Company, based in Washington, D.C. Ms. Nanay is one of the company's directors. This article is the text of Mr. West's testimony before the U.S. Senate Foreign Relations Committee's Subcommittee on International Economic Policy, Export, and Trade Promotion on April 12, 2000.

6.   Ibid., 114.

7.   Ibid., 115.

8.   Ibid., 120–21.

9.   Ibid., 113.

10.   See, for instance, "TCGP's Woes Multiply with Threat of Competing Caspian Gas Export Line," *Oil & Gas Journal*, Online Story, 5 June 2000.

11.   "Shell Still Keen on Trans-Caspian Gas Line," *Oil & Gas Journal*, Online Story, 21 July 2000.

Chapter II: The United States and the Caspian Basin

1.   Deputy Secretary of State Strobe Talbott, "A Farewell to Flashman: American Policy in the Caucasus and Central Asia," Address to the Central Asia-Caucasus Institute at the Nitze School of Advanced International Studies of Johns Hopkins University, Washington, D.C., 21 July 1997.

2.   Laurent Ruseckas, "State of the Field Report: Energy and Politics in Central Asia and the Caucasus," *Access Asia Review* 1, no. 2 (1998): 41–84.

3.   Talbott, op. cit.; Stephen Sestanovich, Statement before the House International Relations Committee, 30 April 1998.

4.   Martha Brill Olcott, "The Caspian's False Promise," *Foreign Policy* 111 (Summer 1998): 101.

5. International Monetary Fund, *Republic of Kazakhstan: Recent Economic Developments,* IMF Staff Country Report No. 98/84 (August 1998): 26, 63.
6. USAID Congressional presentation, www.info.usaid.gov/pubs/cp2000/eni/kazak.html.
7. *The Cyber-Caravan*, 25 January 1999.
8. International Monetary Fund, *Republic of Uzbekistan: Recent Economic Developments*, IMF Staff Country Report No. 98/116 (October 1998): 13. The careful reader will note that these FDI numbers for Uzbekistan are considerably higher than those in Table I-3. As the relevant footnote in the IMF report notes, estimates of foreign direct investment are subject to considerable uncertainty. This footnote mentions lower EBRD estimates that are the same as those in Table I-3.
9. Sestanovich, op. cit.; interviews with former OSCE and UN observers in Georgia.
10. *The Cyber-Caravan*, 25 January 1999.
11. Talbott, op. cit.; Interview with Ambassador Stephen Sestanovich, 15 April 1999.
12. Stuart Eizenstat, Testimony before the U.S. Senate Foreign Relations Committee's International Economic Policy, Export, and Trade Promotion Subcommittee, 23 October 1997.
13. Olcott, op. cit., 111.
14. Eizenstat, op. cit.; interviews with senior Administration officials in May 1999 and January 2000.
15. Olcott, op. cit., 95
16. Presentation to the Standing Committee on Foreign Affairs and International Trade of the House of Commons, 4 April 2000.
17. For instance, Hurricane Hydrocarbons, from its Kumkol field in central Kazakhstan and its Shymkent refinery, provides more than half of Kazakhstan's domestic market for refined products.

Chapter IV: Europe in the New Central Asia

1. The authors of a recent history quote approvingly a note to them from an older authority on Central Asia with whom they had spoken: "In the light of history, I think the Game really was a game, with scores but no substantive prizes." See the note from Harry Hodson quoted in Karl E. Meyer and Shaheen Blair Brysac, *Tournament of Shadows: The Great Game and the Race for Empire in Central Asia* (Washington, D.C.: Counterpoint, 1999), 557 and 573.
2. "The Caucasus: Where Worlds Collide," *The Economist*, 19 August 2000, 18.